AGES 7 to 11

everyday French

A l'école

## IMPORTANT – Permitted use and warnings

Alison Clarke & Heather Crabtree

# Credits and acknowledgements

## Minimum specification

- PC or Mac with CD-ROM drive and 512 Mb RAM (recommended)
- Windows 2000 or above/Mac OSX 10.4
- Recommended minimum processor speed: 1.3 Ghz

**Mixed Sources**
Product group from well-managed forests and other controlled sources
www.fsc.org   Cert no. TT-COC-002769
© 1996 Forest Stewardship Council
FSC

## Acknowledgements

The publishers gratefully acknowledge permission to reproduce the following copyright material:

*Cartes Cochons* for the use of 'L'alphabet Français' from *Allez Hop ! Chantez !* by Alison Middleton and Anne Oliver © 2008, Alison Middleton © (2008, *Cartes Cochons*)

© Crown copyright material. Reproduced under the terms of the Click Use licence.

Every effort has been made to trace copyright holders for the works reproduced in this book, and the publishers apologise for any inadvertent omissions.

Due to the nature of the web, we cannot guarantee the content or links of any site mentioned. We strongly recommend that teachers check websites before using them in the classroom.

**Authors**
Alison Clarke &
Heather Crabtree

**Commissioning Editor**
Juliet Gladston

**Editor**
Tracy Kewley

**Development Editors**
Fabia Lewis, Kate Pedlar
Janet Phillips & Niamh O'Carroll

**Series Designers and Cover Artwork**
Sonja Bagley &
Joy Monkhouse

**Designers**
Shelley Best & Sonja Bagley

**CD-ROM design and development team**
Joy Monkhouse,
Allison Parry, Andrea Lewis,
Anna Oliwa, Shelley Best,
Haremi & Ellosk09 Ltd.

Designed using Adobe Indesign
Published by Scholastic Ltd
Book End, Range Road,
Witney,
Oxfordshire, OX29 OYD
www.scholastic.co.uk

Printed by Bell & Bain Ltd, Glasgow
Text © 2010, Alison Clarke &
Heather Crabtree
© 2010, Scholastic Ltd
1 2 3 4 5 6 7 8 9   0 1 2 3 4 5 6 7 8 9

**British Library Cataloguing-in-Publication Data**
A catalogue record for this book is available from the British Library.
**ISBN 978-1407-10204-7**

# Contents

# Resources on the CD-ROM

**Unit 1**
Interactive flashcard: *Le corps humain*
Interactive activity: *Jacques a dit*
Photocopiable: *Jacques a dit*

**Unit 2**
Interactive flashcard: *Dans mon cartable 1*
Interactive flashcard: *Dans mon cartable 2*
Interactive activity: *Un ou une ?*
Photocopiable: *Mon cartable*
Photocopiable: *Dans mon cartable 1*
Photocopiable: *Dans mon cartable 2*

**Unit 3**
Interactive flashcard: *Qu'est qu'ils aiment faire ?*
Interactive activity: *Ma matière préférée*
Photocopiable: *Mon emploi du temps*
Film: *L'École Jeanne d'Arc*
Transcript: *L'École Jeanne d'Arc*

**Unit 4**
Interactive flashcard: *Calculons ! 1*
Interactive flashcard: *Calculons ! 2*
Interactive flashcard: *Toutes les formes*
Interactive activity: *Je suis quelle forme ?*
Photocopiable: *Coloriez les formes*
Photocopiable: *Les formes et les couleurs*

**Unit 5**
Interactive flashcard: *L'alphabet français*
Interactive activity: *Comment ça s'écrit ?*
Photocopiable: *Le graphisme*
Photocopiable: *L'alphabet français*
Song: *L'alphabet français*

**Unit 6**
Interactive flashcard: *Mon uniforme scolaire*
Interactive activity: *Un, une ou des ?*
Photocopiable: *Les dominos*

**Unit 7**
Interactive flashcard: *Dans ma salle de classe*
Interactive flashcard: *Où est le lapin ?*
Interactive activity: *Dans ma salle de classe*
Photocopiable: *Cache le lapin !*
Photocopiable: *Dans ma salle de classe*

**Unit 8**
Interactive activity: *C'est qui ? 1*
Interactive activity: *C'est qui ? 2*
Photocopiable: *Qu'est-ce qu'ils aiment faire ?*
Photocopiable: *Maths, les maths 1*
Photocopiable: *Maths, les maths 2*
Song: *Maths, les maths*
Translation: *Maths, les maths*

**Unit 9**
Interactive flashcard: *Le nouvel élève*
Interactive activity: *Les règles de l'école*
Photocopiable: *Bienvenue aux scouts*

**Unit 10**
Interactive flashcard: *Quelle heure est-il ? 1*
Interactive flashcard: *Quelle heure est-il ? 2*
Interactive activity: *C'est quel cours ?*
Photocopiable: *Loto*

**Unit 11**
Interactive flashcard: *Notre école*
Interactive activity: *Qu'est-ce qu'on fait ?*
Photocopiable: *Mon école idéale*

**Unit 12**
Interactive flashcard: *Jeux pour la récréation 1*
Interactive flashcard: *Jeux pour la récréation 2*
Interactive flashcard: *Jeux pour la récréation 3*
Interactive flashcard: *Le fermier dans son pré*
Interactive activity: *Jeux pour la récréation*
Photocopiable: *Chansons et jeux pour la récréation*
Translation: *Chansons et jeux pour la récréation*

# Introduction

## Introduction

The activities in this book are intended to be practical and enjoyable while at the same time laying some sound foundations for language learning. Most of the units can be taught independently of the others, while others build on previous units.

On pages 8–9 there is a grid linking the units to the KS2 Framework for Languages indicating the relevant strand and, where appropriate, objective, and using the usual abbreviations:

> O = Oracy
> L = Literacy
> IU = Intercultural understanding
> LLS = Language learning strategies
> KAL = Knowledge about Language

## Introducing new core vocabulary

- Always make sure the children are watching and listening. Get into a routine of saying *Regardez !* (Watch!) – make a spectacles shape with your fingers or point to your eyes; *Écoutez !* (Listen!) – gesture to your ears.
- Choose the simplest phrases to introduce first – especially if they are 'cognates' (look or sound like their English equivalents). This builds confidence!
- Only teach a few phrases at a time – so, to start with, try, for example, *les maths* then *les sciences* and *la géographie*. Play a couple of simple games (see below) then introduce the others.
- Point to/hold up the flashcard as you say the phrase.
- Use gestures to reinforce the meaning – for example, a racquet movement for *le sport*, playing a trumpet for *la musique*.

## Games for practising vocabulary

- **Répétez si c'est vrai** – Hold up a flashcard or object and say a word or phrase. The children repeat only if what the teacher says matches the picture or object she is holding.
- **Secret signal** – Sit the children in a horseshoe shape so that they can see each other. Display all the vocabulary items learned in a clear 'list' form. Choose one child to be the 'detective' who will go outside the room (accompanied by a TA perhaps). Choose another child to be the 'secret signaller'. Explain to the children that you are all going to chant the words/phrases, starting with the one at the beginning of the list. When the secret signaller makes the secret signal (for example, rubbing the forehead or scratching an ear) you will all start chanting the next phrase in the list. The aim of the game is for the secret signaller to avoid detection and for the class to chant the phrases for as long as possible.

# Introduction

- **Quick whizz** – Put picture cards in a pile with their pictures hidden from the class. Make a play of 'shuffling' the cards. Ask the children to say the word or phrase together when they can see what it is. Take the top one and quickly 'whizz' it, picture facing the children, but making it disappear again very quickly. Repeat as many times as you wish. Keep shuffling and emphasising that it's a game. From the teacher's point of view, this game is about getting the children to practise words and phrases; for the children it's about being the fastest and most observant.

- **Fly swat** – You need two plastic flyswats and a set of flashcards fixed to a wall or board with sticky putty. The class is divided into two teams and children take turns to come forward. The teacher calls out a phrase/word. The first person to swat the correct flashcard wins a point for his/her team.

- **Salade de fruits** – The purpose of this game is to get children listening (and responding) to language. The children sit on the floor in a circle. Choose a limited number of vocabulary items. Give each child a word/phrase to remember, so that several children have the same phrase. When the teacher calls out one of the words or phrases the children with that phrase must stand up and change places. Now and then, call out *salade de fruits* and all must change places.

- **Hot/cold** – This game is excellent for whole-class practice of a 'hard to pronounce' word or phrase, such as *Qu'est-ce qu'ils aiment faire à l'école ?* (What do they like to do at school?). The seeker is sent out of the room, while the teacher or child hides the object or flashcard. As the seeker re-enters the room, the class begins to chant the word or phrase repeatedly and rhythmically, getting louder as they get closer, or softer as they move further away, until the object is found.

- **Morpion** (noughts and crosses) – On your class whiteboard, or using an interactive whiteboard, draw a 3 x 3 grid. Stick a word card in each of the squares so that the children can identify their chosen square. Divide the class into two teams – *les cercles* (o) *et les croix* (x). Tell the class: *choisissez une case* (choose a square). Teams take turns to choose a square and a member of the team must say the word on that flashcard to place their nought or cross on the board.

## Introducing the written word

- Make reading cards for new words and phrases, so that you can introduce the written form of the new language you have taught in a planned and systematic way.

- When you show the children new word cards, always get them to read them aloud with you, insisting on correct pronunciation.

- Ask the children to tell you about 'surprises' in the spellings (eg silent *s* or *t* at the ends of words).

- Encourage the children to look out for rhymes and patterns, pointing out which vowels make which sounds in French (eg the letter *i* in *petit*, *il*, *avril* making a sound like the English 'ee').

## The gender of nouns

- You may find it helpful to add a system of colour-coding to the word and picture cards (say, red for feminine, blue for masculine) to help children remember which words are masculine and which words are feminine.

- Always introduce nouns with a definite/indefinite article (eg *le livre, une règle*), never the noun on its own. This will help children to remember the gender of the noun.

# How to use the CD-ROM

Here are brief guidance notes for using the CD-ROM. For more detailed information, see **How to use** on the start-up screen, or **Help** on the relevant screen for information about a particular resource. The CD-ROM follows the structure of the book and contains:

- 12 on-screen interactive activities
- 15 on-screen interactive flashcards
- Audio songs
- Film clips
- Images and poster pages
- All of the photocopiable pages including the song lyrics and English translations

## Getting started

To begin using the CD-ROM, simply place it in your CD- or DVD-ROM drive. Although the CD-ROM should auto run, if it fails to do so, navigate to the drive and double-click on the red **Start** icon.

## Start-up screen

The start-up screen is the first screen that appears. Here you can access: how to use the CD-ROM, terms and conditions, credits and registration links. If you agree to the terms and conditions, click **Start** to continue.

## Main menu

The main menu provides links to all of the Units. Clicking on the relevant Unit icon will take you to the Unit screen where you can access all the Unit's resources. Clicking on **Resource finder** will take you to a search screen for all the resources, where you can search by key word or Unit for a specific resource.

## Resource finder

The **Resource finder** lists all of the resources on the CD-ROM. You can:

- Select a Unit by choosing the appropriate title from the drop-down menu.
- Search for key words by typing them into the search box.
- Scroll up or down the list of resources to locate the required resource.
- Launch a resource by clicking once on its row on the screen.

- Access the glossary of French words and English translations. (See more information below.)

## Navigation

The resources all open in separate windows on top of the menu screen. To close a resource, click on the arrow in the top right-hand corner of the screen. To return to the menu screen you can either close or minimise a resource.

Closing a resource will not close the program. However, if you are in a menu screen, then clicking on the **x** in the top right-hand corner of the screen will close the program. To return to a previous menu screen, you need to click on the **Back** arrow button.

## Glossary

All of the interactive activities and interactive flashcards link to a glossary. The glossary will open in a separate window. Simply click first on the desired headletter and then on the French word to reveal the English translation. You can also click on the audio buttons to hear the pronunciation of each French word.

## Whiteboard tools

The CD-ROM comes with its own set of whiteboard tools for use on any whiteboard. These include:

- Pen tool
- Highlighter tool
- Eraser
- Sticky note

Click on the **Tools** button on the right-hand side of the screen to access these tools.

## Printing

Print the resources by clicking on the **Print** button. The photocopiable pages print as full A4 portrait pages, but please note, if you have a landscape photocopiable page or poster you need to set the orientation to landscape in your print preferences. Printouts of the interactive activities will include what is on the screen. For a full A4 printout you need to set the orientation to landscape in your print preferences.

# Framework links

| Unit | Oracy | Literacy | Knowledge about language | IU | Language and learning strategies |
|---|---|---|---|---|---|
| 1 | 3.1, 3.2, 3.3, 3.4, 4.1, 4.2, 5.3, 5.4, 6.4 | 3.1, 3.2, 4.1, 4.3, 5.2, 6.1 | **Year 3:** Identify specific sounds, phonemes and words; recognise question forms and negatives; recognise how sounds are represented in written form; notice the spelling of familiar words; recognise conventions of politeness. **Year 4:** Reinforce and extend recognition of word classes and understand their function; apply phonic knowledge of the language to support reading and writing. **Year 5:** Recognise patterns in simple sentences; manipulate language by changing an element in a sentence. **Year 6:** Recognise patterns in the foreign language. | 6.3 | • Use actions and rhymes and play games to aid memorisation. • Practise new language with a friend. • Look at the face of the person speaking and listen attentively. • Notice the spelling of familiar words. • Use context and previous knowledge to determine meaning and pronunciation. • Read and memorise words. • Listen for clues to meaning eg tone of voice, key words. |
| 2 | 3.2, 3.3, 3.4, 4.2, 4.3, 4.4, 5.1, 5.3, 5.4, 6.4 | 3.1, 3.2, 4.1, 4.3, 4.4, 5.2, 5.3, 6.3 | **Year 3:** Identify specific sounds, phonemes and words; imitate pronunciation of sounds; hear main word classes; recognise question forms and negatives. **Year 4:** Reinforce and extend recognition of word classes and understand their function; use question forms. **Year 5:** Recognise patterns in simple sentences; manipulate language by changing an element in a sentence; recognise the typical conventions of word order in the foreign language. **Year 6:** Recognise patterns in the foreign language; use knowledge of words, text and structure to build simple spoken and written passages. | | • Discuss language learning and share ideas and experiences. • Use actions and rhymes and play games to aid memorisation. • Practise new language with a friend. • Recognise words which the teacher mouths silently. • Read and memorise words. • Sort words into categories. • Apply grammatical knowledge to make sentences. • Use a dictionary or word list. • Compare and reflect on techniques for memorising language. |
| 3 | 3.2, 3.3, 4.1, 4.4, 5.1, 5.2, 6.4 | 3.1, 3.2, 3.3, 4.1, 4.3, 4.4, 5.1, 5.2, 5.3, 6.1, 6.3 | **Year 3:** Identify specific sounds, phonemes and words; imitate pronunciation of sounds; hear main word classes; recognise question forms and negatives. **Year 4:** Reinforce and extend knowledge of word classes and understand their function. **Year 5:** Recognise patterns in simple sentences; manipulate language by changing an element in a sentence; understand and use negatives. **Year 6:** Notice and match agreements; use knowledge of words, text and structure to build spoken and written passages. | 3.3, 3.4, 4.1, 4.2, 5.1, 6.2 | • Use actions and rhymes and play games to aid memorisation. • Use the context of what they see/read to determine some of the meaning. • Write new words. • Compare the language with English. • Practise new language with a friend. • Read and memorise words. |
| 4 | 3.2, 3.3, 3.4, 4.1, 4.2, 4.3, 5.1, 6.4 | 3.1, 3.2, 4.2, 4.3, 5.2, 6.3 | **Year 3:** Imitate pronunciation of sounds; recognise question forms and negatives; recognise how sounds are represented in written form. **Year 4:** Use question forms; apply phonic knowledge of the language to support reading and writing. **Year 5:** Manipulate language by changing an element in a sentence; apply knowledge of rules when building sentences. **Year 6:** Use knowledge of word and text conventions to build sentences and short texts; devise questions for authentic use. | | • Use actions and rhymes and play games to aid memorisation. • Use gestures to show they understand. • Read and memorise words. • Apply knowledge of rules when building sentences. |
| 5 | 3.1, 3.2, 3.3, 3.4, 4.1, 4.2, 4.3, 5.1, 6.4 | 3.1, 3.2, 3.3, 4.2, 4.3, 5.2, 5.3, 6.3 | **Year 3:** Identify specific sounds, phonemes and words; recognise commonly used rhyming sounds; imitate pronunciation of sounds; recognise how sounds are represented in written form; notice the spelling of familiar words. **Year 4:** Identify a different writing system. **Year 5:** Manipulate language by changing an element in a sentence; develop accuracy in pronunciation and intonation; appreciate that different languages use different writing conventions. **Year 6:** Use knowledge of words, text and structure to build simple spoken and written passages. | 3.3, 4.2, 4.3, 5.1, 6.2, 6.3 | • Use actions and rhymes and play games to aid memorisation. • Practise new language with a friend. • Compare the language with English. • Read and memorise words. • Look and listen for visual and aural clues. |
| 6 | 3.2, 3.3, 4.2, 4.4, 5.2, 5.4, 6.1, 6.2, 6.4 | 3.1, 3.2, 3.3, 4.1, 4.3, 5.2, 5.3, 6.3 | **Year 3:** Hear main word classes, recognise question forms and negatives; recognise that languages describe familiar things differently. **Year 4:** Reinforce and extend recognition of word classes and understand their function; apply phonic knowledge of the language to support reading and writing. **Year 5:** Recognise patterns in simple sentences; understand and use negatives. **Year 6:** Recognise patterns in the foreign language; notice and match agreements. | 3.3, 3.4, 4.2, 5.1, 6.1, 6.2 | • Discuss language learning and share ideas and experiences. • Use actions and rhymes and play games to aid memorisation. • Practise new language with a friend. • Use mental associations to help remember words. • Ask for repetition and clarification. • Read and memorise words. • Sort words into categories. • Use a dictionary. |

| Unit | Oracy | Literacy | Knowledge about language | IU | Language and learning strategies |
|---|---|---|---|---|---|
| 7 | 3.2, 3.3, 3.4<br>4.2, 4.3, 4.4<br>5.1, 5.4<br>6.3, 6.4 | 3.1, 3.2, 3.3<br>4.1, 4.3, 4.4<br>5.2, 5.3<br>6.3 | **Year 3:** Identify specific sounds, phonemes and words; imitate pronunciation of sounds; hear main word classes; notice the spelling of familiar words.<br>**Year 4:** Use question forms.<br>**Year 5:** Recognise patterns in simple sentences; manipulate language by changing an element in a sentence; understand and use negatives.<br>**Year 6:** Recognise patterns in the foreign language. | | • Use actions and rhymes and play games to aid memorisation.<br>• Practise new language with a friend.<br>• Look at the face of the person speaking and listen attentively.<br>• Write new words.<br>• Use mental associations to help remember words.<br>• Read and memorise words.<br>• Use a dictionary.<br>• Look and listen for visual and aural clues. |
| 8 | 3.1, 3.2, 3.3,<br>3.4<br>4.1, 4.2, 4.4<br>5.3, 5.4<br>6.1, 6.3, 6.4 | 3.1, 3.2, 3.3,<br>3.4<br>4.1, 4.2, 4.4<br>5.2, 5.3<br>6.1, 6.3, 6.4 | **Year 3:** Identify specific sounds, phonemes and words; recognise commonly used rhyming sounds; imitate pronunciation of sounds.<br>**Year 4:** Recognise and apply simple agreements, singular and plural; apply phonic knowledge of the language to support reading and writing.<br>**Year 5:** Recognise patterns in simple sentences; manipulate language by changing an element in a sentence; use knowledge of words, text and structure to build simple spoken and written passages; use knowledge of word and text conventions to build sentences and short texts.<br>**Year 6:** Recognise patterns in the foreign language; use knowledge of word and text conventions to build sentences. | 6.3 | • Use actions and rhymes and play games to aid memorisation.<br>• Remember rhyming words.<br>• Use the context of what they see/hear to determine some of the meaning.<br>• Use mental associations to help remember words.<br>• Use context and previous knowledge to determine meaning and pronunciation.<br>• Apply a range of linguistic knowledge to create simple, written production. |
| 9 | 3.2, 3.4<br>4.1, 4.2<br>5.3, 5.4<br>6.2, 6.3 | 3.1, 3.2, 3.3<br>4.1, 4.2<br>5.1, 5.2<br>6.1, 6.3 | **Year 3:** Identify specific sounds, phonemes and words; hear main word classes; recognise how sounds are represented in written form; notice the spelling of familiar words.<br>**Year 4:** Apply phonic knowledge of the language to support reading and writing.<br>**Year 5:** Recognise patterns in simple sentences; manipulate language by changing an element in a sentence.<br>**Year 6:** Recognise patterns in the foreign language; use knowledge of word order and sentence construction to support the understanding of the written text; use knowledge of word and text conventions to build sentences and short texts. | | • Discuss language learning and share ideas and experiences.<br>• Use actions and rhymes and play games to aid memorisation.<br>• Write new words. • Compare the language with English.<br>• Use mental associations to help remember words.<br>• Use context and previous knowledge to determine meaning and pronunciation.<br>• Plan and prepare for a language activity. • Read and memorise words.<br>• Sort words into categories. • Use a dictionary.<br>• Use language known in one context or topic in another context or topic. |
| 10 | 3.2, 3.2, 3.4<br>4.1, 4.2<br>5.1, 5.4<br>6.4 | 3.1, 3.3<br>4.3, 4.4<br>5.3<br>6.3 | **Year 3:** Identify specific sounds, phonemes and words; imitate pronunciation of sounds; recognise question forms and negatives; recognise that languages describe familiar things differently.<br>**Year 4:** Reinforce and extend recognition of word classes and understand their function; use question forms.<br>**Year 5:** Recognise patterns in simple sentences; understand and use negatives.<br>**Year 6:** Recognise patterns in the foreign language; use knowledge of word and text conventions to build sentences and short texts. | | • Use actions and rhymes and play games to aid memorisation.<br>• Practise new language with a friend.<br>• Write new words.<br>• Compare the language with English.<br>• Read and memorise words. |
| 11 | 3.2, 3.3, 3.4<br>4.2, 4.4<br>5.1, 5.2, 5.3,<br>5.4<br>6.2, 6.4 | 3.1, 3.3<br>4.1, 4.3, 4.4<br>5.2, 5.3<br>6.3, 6.4 | **Year 3:** Hear main word classes; recognise question forms and negatives; notice the spelling of familiar words.<br>**Year 4:** Reinforce and extend recognition of word classes and understand their function; use question forms.<br>**Year 5:** Recognise patterns in simple sentences; manipulate language by changing an element in a sentence; apply knowledge of rules when building sentences; understand and use negatives.<br>**Year 6:** Recognise patterns in the foreign language; notice and match agreements; use knowledge of words, text and structure to build simple spoken and written passages; use knowledge of word and text conventions to build sentences and short texts. | 3.4<br>6.3 | • Discuss language learning and share ideas and experiences.<br>• Practise new language with a friend.<br>• Recognise words that the teacher mouths silently.<br>• Write new words.<br>• Compare the language with English.<br>• Plan and prepare for a language activity.<br>• Read and memorise words.<br>• Apply knowledge about letters and simple grammatical knowledge to experiment with writing. • Use a dictionary. |
| 12 | 3.1, 3.2, 3.3,<br>3.4<br>4.1, 4.2, 4.3<br>5.3<br>6.1, 6.2 | 3.1, 3.2, 3.3<br>4.1, 4.2, 4.4<br>5.1, 5.3<br>6.1, 6.2 | **Year 3:** Identify specific sounds, phonemes and words; recognise commonly used rhyming sounds; imitate pronunciation of sounds; recognise how sounds are represented in written form; notice the spelling of familiar words.<br>**Year 4:** Recognise that texts in other languages will often have the same conventions of style and layout.<br>**Year 5:** Recognise patterns in simple sentences; apply knowledge of rules when building sentences.<br>**Year 6:** Recognise patterns in the foreign language; notice and match agreements. | 3.4<br>6.3 | • Use actions and rhymes and play games to aid memorisation.<br>• Remember rhyming words.<br>• Practise new language with a friend and outside the classroom.<br>• Recognise words which the teacher mouths silently.<br>• Write new words. • Read and memorise words.<br>• Look and listen for visual and aural clues.<br>• Pronounce/read aloud unknown words. |

# Unit 1: Jacques a dit

## Objective

**To learn basic classroom instructions in French.**

## Introducing the vocabulary

- Use photocopiable page 34 (*Jacques a dit*) to introduce classroom commands two or three at a time. Say the phrase and ask the children to make the correct actions. At this point they should listen carefully (*écoutez bien*) but not repeat what you say (*ne répétez pas*).
- Once the children know six to eight different phrases, you can use some of them to play *Jacques a dit*, the French equivalent of 'Simon says'. The children must only carry out the command if you say '*Jacques a dit*'. Tell them '*Écoutez bien. Regardez-moi. Si je dis 'Jacques a dit', faites le geste. Si je ne dis pas 'Jacques a dit', ne faites pas le geste !*' Anyone who makes a mistake is out (*éliminé*).

## Core activities

- Give pairs of children sets of cards made from photocopiable page 34 (*Jacques a dit*). Call out a command in French and ask the children to take it in turns to hold up the correct card. Repeat a few times. This will allow you to see which children have grasped the new phrases. Next call out sequences of two, then three and even four commands and challenge the children to hold up the cards in the correct order.
- Use photocopiable page 34 (*Jacques a dit*) again to practise pronunciation of the phrases. This time tell the children *Écoutez bien et répétez.*
- Let the children practise the phrases in pairs. First, one child should give a command while the other child shows the correct card. Then one child should do an action while the other responds with a spoken command. This could also be done in small groups. While the class works on this activity, let children take turns to complete 'Interactive activity: *Jacques a dit*' from the CD-ROM.
- Display the large version of the cards. Ask the children what they notice about the sounds and spellings of the words. They should tell you that there is a silent *z* at the end of each command. They may also notice the *sh* sound of the *ch* in *touchez*, the silent *s* in *vous* and the silent *x* in *yeux*.

## Extension activities

- Now that the children understand *fermez/ouvrez les yeux*, you can introduce and use *fermez/ouvrez ... la porte/ la fenêtre/les cahiers/les livres*.
- Use 'Interactive flashcard: *Le corps humain*' from the CD-ROM to learn or revise some parts of the body and encourage the children to use these in their own *Jacques a dit* games. (See also 'Five-minute follow-ups'.)
- Gradually introduce the singular form of the imperative into your games and activities (see Key phrases – Extension), for example: *Assieds-toi, Martin ! Ouvre la porte, Sophie !* If this is used in an informal way, where the meaning will be obvious, the children will soon understand that you are addressing just one person. In the future you can discuss and analyse this. Don't forget to add *s'il vous plaît* or *s'il te plaît* (please).

## Cross-curricular ideas

**PE: To play warm-up games in French.**

Incorporate some energetic commands into PE warm-ups: *touchez le mur* (touch the wall), *touchez le plancher* (touch the floor), *courez* (run), *sautez* (jump), *sautillez* (skip), *marchez* (walk), *dansez* (dance).

### Resources

Interactive flashcard:
*Le corps humain*

Interactive activity:
*Jacques a dit*

Photocopiable page 34:
*Jacques a dit*

### Preparation

Sets of cards made from photocopiable page 34 (*Jacques a dit*), enough for one per pair, and an enlarged set of cards for display

Interactive whiteboard

## Tips

Use commands in French at the start and end of lessons, when the children are lining up and generally to get their attention. Build on them and embed them into other curriculum areas, for example: *prenez les ciseaux* (take the scissors), *coupez* (cut), *pliez* (fold), *dessinez* (draw), *calculez* (calculate).

# Five-minute follow-ups

- Learn and sing the French version of 'Heads, Shoulders, Knees and Toes' (to the same tune). Note that the French version refers to feet rather than toes.

  *La tête, les épaules, les genoux, les doigts de pied*
  *Les genoux, les doigts de pieds*
  *La tête, les épaules, les genoux, les doigts de pied*
  *Les genoux, les doigts de pied*
  *Les yeux, les oreilles, la bouche, le nez*
  *La tête, les épaules, les genoux, les doigts de pied*

- Teach the children's song *Jean Petit qui Danse*. You will find the words, music and even video clips of this popular, traditional song if you type the song title into your search engine.

## Key words

### Core:

*éliminé* – out (of the game)
*la table* – the table
*la main* – the (your) hand
*les yeux* (m) – the (your) eyes
*prenez* – take
*coupez* – cut
*pliez* – fold
*dessinez* – draw
*calculez* – calculate
(The plural/polite form of the imperative is given here.)

### Extension:

*la porte* – the door
*la fenêtre* – the window
*les cahiers* (m) – the (your) exercise books
*les livres* (m) – the books
*le corps humain* (m) – the human body
*la tête* – the (your) head
*les épaules* (f) – the (your) shoulders
*le genou* – the (your) knee
*les pieds* (m) – the (your) feet
*les oreilles* (f) – the (your) ears
*la bouche* – the (your) mouth
*le nez* – the (your) nose

## Key phrases

### Core:

*'Jacques a dit'* – 'Simon says' (literally 'James said')
*écoutez bien* – listen carefully
*regardez-moi* – look at me
*faites le geste* – do the gesture
*ne répétez pas* – do not repeat
*levez la main* – raise your hand
*baissez la main* – lower your hand
*levez-vous* – get up/stand up
*asseyez-vous* – sit down
*touchez la table* – touch the table
*fermez les yeux* – close your eyes
*ouvrez les yeux* – open your eyes
*taisez-vous* – be quiet
(The plural/polite form of the imperative is given here.)

### Extension:

*écoute !* – listen !
*lève (la main)* – raise (your hand)
*baisse (la main)* – lower (your hand)
*lève-toi* – stand up
*assieds-toi* – sit down
*touche (le genou)* – touch (your knee)
*ferme (la porte)* – close (the door)
*ouvre (la fenêtre)* – open (the window)
*tais-toi !* – be quiet!
(The singular/informal form of the imperative is given above.)
*s'il te plaît/s'il vous plaît* – please
*courez* – run
*sautez* – jump
*sautillez* – skip
*marchez* – walk
*dansez* – dance

## Language points

- The key language of this unit is the imperative (command) form of some common verbs. Because teachers will be working with groups of children we use the plural command for the core activities. The imperative is normally formed from the *vous* part of the present tense of the verb. There is no need to explain this to the children at this stage.

# Unit 2: Dans mon cartable ...

## Objective

**To learn the vocabulary for items in the class; to learn about the indefinite article (un/une/des).**

## Introducing the vocabulary

- Open 'Interactive flashcard: *Dans mon cartable 1*' from the CD-ROM. Look at the masculine items. Click on the items one by one to hear their names in French. Ask the children to listen and repeat.

- Give the children sets of picture cards made from the photocopiable pages from the CD-ROM. Say the name of an item and ask the children to hold up the picture.

- Show the children the school bag you have prepared and pull out only masculine nouns at this point. Ask: *C'est un ...?* The children should reply *oui* or *non*. Then move on to two-part questions, for example: *C'est un bic ou c'est un livre ?* The children should reply with one of the words. Finally, ask *Qu'est-ce que c'est ?* and ask the children to respond with *C'est un/une ...* If they don't use the article repeat the answer for them, inserting the article.

- Look at 'Interactive flashcard: *Dans mon cartable 2*' from the CD-ROM and give the children sets of picture cards made from the photocopiable pages, as above. Introduce the feminine items in the same way as before. Leave out the plurals (*des ciseaux* and *des feutres*) at this stage. Take the real items out of the bag and use different voices to introduce and practise the words. Mouth the item silently and challenge the children to guess which word it is.

## Core activities

- Ask the children to choose one picture and put it behind their backs. Say all the masculine and feminine nouns. Children should listen but only repeat the word when it is the item they are holding.

- Ask the children to get up and move around, telling each other what their item is using *J'ai un/une ...* After a while say 'Stop'. The children must quickly find a partner who has a different item. The pairs then mingle together, this time saying both items to all pairs that they meet. When you say 'Stop' they need to find another pair who have different items. Ask the children to say their words to each other once more. When they have done this say to them: *Mettez-vous en ordre alphabétique*. The first group to get into alphabetical order raises their hands and then says their words to the rest of the class.

- Show the children the slinky. Squeeze it together and say *un* then stretch it apart and say *une*. Ask for volunteers to take an item out of the bag and say the item's name, using the slinky to show whether it is *un* or *une*.

- Discuss language learning strategies. Sometimes it can be easier to learn words if they are grouped together. Give the children copies of photocopiable page 35 (*Mon cartable*) and ask them to cut out the words. Give them five minutes to work out any groups and ways in which they might remember this new vocabulary. Suggest that they use the picture cards as well.

- Ask the children to cut out the school bag from the photocopiable page and to stick the pictures of items that they'd like to put in their bag on the front. They should stick the words for the items on the back. They could use a dictionary to add other items to their bags.

## Extension activities

- Ask the children to put the slinky into the *un* or *une* position and pull out an item lucky-dip style. The rest of the class have to say the word and decide if it fits with the chosen slinky position using 'thumbs-up' or 'thumbs-down'. Confident pupils could try using *Oui, c'est un livre* or *Non, ce n'est pas une livre, c'est un livre*.

---

## Resources

Interactive flashcards:
*Dans mon cartable 1*
*Dans mon cartable 2*

Interactive activity:
*Un ou une ?*

Photocopiable page 35:
*Mon cartable*

Photocopiables:
*Dans mon cartable 1*
*Dans mon cartable 2*

## Preparation

Sets of picture cards made from 'Photocopiables: *Dans mon cartable 1* and *2*', enough for one set per child

A school bag containing the items in the Key words list

A 'slinky' or large spring

Interactive whiteboard

# Unit 2: Dans mon cartable ...

○ Go back to 'Interactive flashcard: *Dans mon cartable*' from the CD-ROM and introduce the remaining two items of vocabulary. Elicit from the pupils that these words are plural and therefore start in a different way.

## Cross-curricular ideas

**Art and design: To create a still-life composition of new vocabulary.**

Ask the children to do a painting in the style of a still-life composition using classroom items. They could hide the French words somewhere in the picture for others to find.

**ICT: To use ICT to help remember vocabulary.**

Following on from your discussion about what can help us to remember vocabulary, challenge the children to use multimedia software to link the French words to a memory trigger such as an image or a sound. They could also experiment with using different fonts, to see if this helps them to commit words to memory.

## Five-minute follow-ups

○ Let the children play games such as snap or Pelmanism (pairs) with the word and picture cards.

○ Let the children complete 'Interactive activity: *Un ou une ?*' from the CD-ROM. They need to decide whether the words are masculine or feminine and drag and drop them into the appropriate box.

## Tips

Add a Language Learning Strategies section to your display board and encourage the children to add suggestions.

Accurate pronunciation of the French *u* sound in *une* is difficult. One way is to get children to say the English sound ee then continue to say it as they purse their lips. The sound that they arrive at when lips are fully pursed will be similar to French *u*.

---

**Key words**

**Core:**

*un cartable* – a school bag
*un bic* – a ballpoint pen
*un livre* – a book
*un cahier* – an exercise book
*un crayon* – a pencil
*un taille-crayon* – a pencil sharpener
*une trousse* – a pencil case
*une règle* – a ruler
*une gomme* – a rubber
*une calculette* – a calculator
*des feutres* (m) – felt pens/board pens
*des ciseaux* (m) – scissors
*ou* – or

**Key phrases**

**Core:**

*dans mon cartable* – in my school bag
*C'est un/une ...* – It's a...
*Qu'est-ce que c'est ?* – What is it?
*J'ai* – I have
*Mettez-vous en ordre alphabétique* – Put yourselves in alphabetical order

**Extension:**

*Ce n'est pas un/une ...* – It isn't a...

---

**Language points**

○ In this unit we begin to focus on the notion of gender. All nouns in French are either masculine or feminine and should always be taught with an article which shows gender eg *le/un/mon*. You may want to discuss the fact that many other European languages have this notion of gender. Colour-coding all vocabulary used and using these colours consistently can help to reinforce which group nouns belong to.

# Unit 3: Ma matière préférée

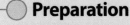 **Resources**

Interactive flashcard:
*Qu'est qu'ils aiment faire ?*

Interactive activity:
*Ma matière préférée*

Photocopiable page 36:
*Mon emploi du temps*

Film:
*L'Ecole Jeanne d'Arc*

Transcript:
*L'Ecole Jeanne d'Arc*

## Preparation

Word cards showing
days of the week

Interactive whiteboard

## Objectives

**To learn the names of school subjects in French and to express opinions about them; to learn about schools in France and to discuss similarities and differences with schools in the UK.**

## Introducing the vocabulary

- Use 'Interactive flashcard: *Qu'est qu'ils aiment faire ?*' from the CD-ROM to introduce the school subjects and the words *aime*, *n'aime pas* and *déteste*. Click on the pictures to hear sentences in French. Play them several times then check the children's understanding. Discuss which words are close to English equivalents (eg *l'histoire*, *les maths*, *la géographie*). Can the children guess why this might be? (Same Latin roots; common European history.)

## Core activities

- Revise (or teach) the days of the week using word cards. Make a human sequence with one child holding each day's card then chant the days rhythmically as a class.

- Give the children a copy each of photocopiable page 36 (*Mon emploi du temps*). Ask if anyone can guess the meaning of the following words and phrases: *mon emploi du temps*, *le matin*, *l'après-midi*, *la récréation*, *le déjeuner*.

- When the children are confident with the vocabulary for school subjects, ask them to work in pairs to complete the timetable on photocopiable page 36 (*Mon emploi du temps*) based on their own class timetable. They should hold their discussion in French using phrases such as: *L'anglais, c'est lundi matin* ; *L'histoire, c'est vendredi après midi* and so on.

- Discuss the children's results and create a larger version of your class timetable on the interactive whiteboard or a sheet of paper. Use the phrase *C'est juste ?* (Is it correct?) to check that everything is in the right place.

- Talk to the children about primary school in France. School is mandatory from the age of six and children go to primary school (*l'école primaire* or *l'école élémentaire*) between the ages of six and eleven. Children study a range of subjects including science, arts and humanities, but the focus in the primary years is on literacy and numeracy. There is no religious education (*l'éducation religieuse*) in state schools as religion is considered completely separate from the state. The school day in France is longer than in the UK, typically starting at 8.30am and finishing at 4.30pm, but children do not go to school on Wednesdays. French schools have longer holidays: the summer break is two months long and there are two-week holidays in late October, at Christmas, in February and at Easter.

- Explain the importance of *le déjeuner* in France. It is still a main meal often comprising meat with pasta and a salad. Yogurt and fruit are popular desserts. Most children will have a two- or three-course cooked meal at school and the lunch period at school normally lasts for two hours.

- Watch the 'Film: *L'Ecole Jeanne d'Arc*' from the CD-ROM to see a typical day in a French school. Consider the timings of events. How does this compare to your school? What other similarities and differences can the children see? Interesting areas for discussion could be: the children's arrival at/departure from school, lesson style (eg use of whiteboards and flashcards), lunch. Children may also bring up the issue of school uniform. Discuss this briefly and explain that you will be exploring this in more detail in Unit 6.

## Extension activities

- Let the children complete 'Interactive activity: *Ma matière préférée*' from the CD-ROM, which introduces the third-person form '*Il/elle aime ...*' etc. They should select words from the drop-down list to complete the sentences.

- More confident children could hold a discussion about the children featured in 'Interactive flashcard: *Qu'est qu'ils aiment faire à l'école ?*' from the CD-ROM using the third person *il/elle aime/n'aime pas/déteste ...* They could form questions using *Il/elle aime ... ?* with rising intonation.

## Tips

*Etre et Avoir* is a delightful film made in 2002 which documents a year in a tiny Auvergne primary school. It provides an excellent glimpse of a very rural school, its curriculum still strongly focused on literacy and numeracy, but with a unique humanity thanks to the teacher. DVDs of the film are available to rent or buy online.

The French Entrée website (**www.frenchentree.com/fe-education**) has a comprehensive section on the French education system and the French embassy website has some pages aimed at children – **www.ambafrance-uk.org/Look-at-France-A-day-in-the-life.html**

## Cross-curricular ideas

**Maths: To collect, organise and present data about class preferences.**

Ask the children to work in pairs to conduct a survey asking: *Quelle est ta matière préférée ?* They can then use the data to produce a simple pictogram, bar or pie chart, either on paper or using ICT.

## Five-minute follow-ups

- If children have learned the French alphabet (see Unit 5), challenge them to spell out the lessons they will have that morning/afternoon. Get a good rhythm going. Ask the children *C'est quelle leçon maintenant ?* (Which lesson is it now?) Have the word written up on the board. Encourage the children to chant the spelling as they clap the rhythm.
- Play *Morpion* (noughts and crosses, see Introduction) with school subjects and like/dislike symbols. The children should say, for example, *j'aime + la géographie* to indicate where on the grid they would like to put their nought or cross.

### Key words

*l'école primaire/ l'école élémentaire* – primary school
*l'éducation religieuse* (f) – RE
*lundi* – Monday
*mardi* – Tuesday
*mercredi* – Wednesday
*jeudi* – Thursday
*vendredi* – Friday
*samedi* – Saturday
*dimanche* – Sunday
*emploi* (m) *du temps* – timetable
*le matin* – morning
*l'après-midi* (m) – afternoon
*la récréation* – playtime/break
*le déjeuner* – lunch

#### Extension:

*génial* – great
*super* – great, super
*intéressant* – interesting
*difficile* – difficult

### Key words

#### Core:

*les maths* (f) – maths
*les sciences* (f) – science
*le français* – French
*l'anglais* (m) – English
*l'histoire* (f) – history
*la géographie* – geography
*l'informatique* (f) – ICT
*le sport* – PE
*le dessin* – art
*la musique* – music

### Key phrases

#### Core:

*l'anglais, c'est lundi matin* – English is on Monday mornings
*C'est juste ?* – Is that right?
*Quelle est ta leçon/ta matière préférée ?* – What is your favourite lesson/subject?
*C'est* – It is
*Pourquoi ?* – Why?
*j'aime (calculer/chanter)* – I like (doing sums/singing)
*je n'aime pas (parler anglais)* – I don't like (speaking English)
*parce que* – because
*c'est (difficile)* – it's (difficult)

#### Extension:

*Qu'est-ce qu'ils aiment faire à l'école ?* – What do they like doing at school?
*Il/elle adore* – He/she loves
*Il/elle déteste* – He/she hates
*Il/elle n'aime pas* – He /she doesn't like

### Language points

- When expressing likes and dislikes in French remember to include the definite article (*le/la/l'/les*), for example: *j'aime les frites* (I like chips), *j'adore les films du farwest* (I love westerns).

# Unit 4: J'aime les maths !

## Objective

**To perform simple mathematical operations and learn words for shape, size and colour in French.**

## Introducing the vocabulary

- Use 'Interactive flashcard: *Calculons ! 1*' from the CD-ROM to introduce the four maths operations. 'Interactive flashcard: *Calculons ! 2*' uses the vocabulary in the context of numbers to ten. Practise pronunciation, encouraging a good *u* sound for *plus,* at the same time making a vertical/horizontal cross with your fingers. Say *moins* repeatedly (with a good nasal twang), pretending to rub your eyes. You will find yourself making a 'crying' sound. Make a diagonal cross with fingers when you say *fois*. For *divisé par* sketch the horizontal line with two dots in the air.

- Use 'Interactive flashcard: *Toutes les formes*' from the CD-ROM to introduce shapes and colours. Ask the children which words sound like their English equivalents. Encourage them to draw the shapes in the air as they say them to aid memorisation.

## Core activities

- Revise the numbers one to ten using the number cards then try some simple addition sums, initially just orally, then using mini whiteboards. Make a habit of saying *Un, deux, trois ... montrez-moi !* (One, two, three...show me!) so that they all show you their boards at the same time, allowing you to assess their understanding.

- Move on to subtraction, multiplication and division in a similar way. Don't try to introduce all four operations at once.

- Using 0–9 number fans or equivalent cards, ask the children to show you the product of a calculation eg *deux plus trois font ...?*

- Give each group of children a set of 2D shapes. Play *Un, deux, trois ... montrez-moi !*

- On a big sheet of paper draw several shape sequences and keep a note of the sequences you have drawn, for example: *un cercle, un carré, deux rectangles*. Display the sheet of paper but cover it with another sheet so that you can slowly reveal the answers one by one. Ask the children in pairs to draw the sequences of shapes as you read them out. Start simply and get more complex as appropriate.

- Ask the children to continue this exercise in pairs, taking turns to give each other a shape sequence and drawing them on their mini whiteboards. They should check each others' sequences and decide: *C'est juste ou ce n'est pas juste ?* (Is it correct or incorrect?)

- Use the word cards on 'Photocopiable: *Les formes et les couleurs*' from the CD-ROM to build phrases. Hold up a coloured shape and ask the children to work in pairs to find the correct words to make and say the phrase, for example: *C'est un carré rouge.* The children can then work in pairs to challenge each other.

- Let the children practise the shape and colour vocabulary with 'Interactive activity: *Je suis quelle forme ?*' from the CD-ROM. They will need to know the words *un angle* and *un côté*. Introduce these words by showing them a square or a rectangle and saying *J'ai quatre angles et quatre côtés*. Can the children guess the meaning of the words?

## Extension activities

- Give the children a copy each of photocopiable page 37 (*Coloriez les formes*). Ask them to follow the instructions in French, asking for clarification where required. As the children do the task, go round the class asking *Qu'est-ce que tu fais ?* and encouraging them to use phrases such as *Je colorie les triangles en vert; Je fais une voiture*.

- Introduce *un grand carré/un grand cercle/un petit carré/un petit cercle*. Practise *grand/petit* with some examples: *Un éléphant, c'est petit ou grand ?; Un insecte, c'est petit ou grand ?* Ask the children to draw in the air *un petit cercle/un grand cercle/un petit triangle/un grand triangle* and so on.

## Tips

Plastic foam pocket dice are an excellent resource. Use them to practise numbers, shapes, colours and so on. Make your own dice, starting with pictures or symbols, but using French words sometimes for additional challenge.

## Cross-curricular ideas

**Maths: To perform mental calculations in French.**
Once the children are confident with numbers up to 20 and the four operations in French, try mental-maths starters to numeracy lessons in French. Once the children are familiar with a wider range of numbers, you can practise tables in French.

**PE: To carry out warm-up exercises, following instructions in French.**
Ask the children to make a large circle, triangle or square by stretching their arms and legs (*Dessinez un cercle, un triangle* etc). Alternatively, play corners. Place shape cards in each corner of the hall. Children must run to the shape when it is called. Increase the challenge by using the same shape, but in varied colours, sizes or both.

## Five-minute follow-ups

- Let the children draw shapes or write numbers on each others' backs and guess the answers in French. This can be done as a team line game.
- As a follow-up to the interactive activity, play *Je suis quelle forme ?* Describe a shape and let the children guess what it is: *J'ai six côtés* (I have six sides); *J'ai trois angles* (I have three angles).
- Use a large dice to practise number bonds up to ten. Roll the dice. A child says the uppermost number in French eg *quatre*. The rest of the class must write its number bond pair (*six*) on their mini whiteboards. At your signal they show their numbers and say the number in French.

## Key words

### Core:

*plus* – plus
*moins* – minus
*fois* – times
*divisé par* – divided by
*un carré* – a square
*un cercle* – a circle
*un hexagone* – a hexagon
*un rectangle* – a rectangle
*un triangle* – a triangle
*bleu(e)* – blue
*brun(e)* – brown
*jaune* – yellow
*rouge* – red
*vert(e)* – green
*une forme* – a shape
*une couleur* – a colour
*un angle* – an angle
*un côté* – a side
*calculez* – calculate

### Extension:

*grand(e)* – large
*petit(e)* – small
*un éléphant* – an elephant
*un insecte* – an insect
*découpez* – cut out
*coloriez* – colour
*dessinez* – draw

## Key phrases

### Core:

*Un, deux, trois ... montrez-moi !* – One, two, three...show me!
*(Deux plus trois) font (cinq)* – (Two plus three) make (five)
*C'est juste (ou ce n'est pas juste) ?* – Is that correct (or incorrect)?
*Je suis quelle forme ?* – What shape am I?

### Extension:

*toutes les formes* – all the shapes
*Qu'est-ce que tu fais ?* – What are you doing?
*Je colorie (les triangles)* – I am colouring (the triangles)
*Je fais (une voiture)* – I am making (a car)
*un grand carré vert* – a large green square
*un petit triangle bleu* – a small blue triangle
*divisé par ... /multiplié par ...* – divided by.../multiplied by...

## Language points

- In French, most adjectives follow the noun. A few very commonly used adjectives, such as *petit* and *grand,* precede the noun (*un petit triangle bleu*). There are also a few adjectives whose meanings change according to their position in the sentence. One example is *propre* : *les mains propres* means 'clean hands', *mes propres mains* means 'my own hands'.

# Unit 5: L'alphabet et le graphisme

## Objectives

**To explore the sounds of the French alphabet; to learn about the cultural importance of handwriting in French schools.**

## Introducing the vocabulary

- Use 'Interactive flashcard: *L'alphabet français*' from the CD_ROM to introduce the alphabet. Practise the sounds, especially the letters highlighted as these sound very different from their English equivalents. Ask the children to 'notice' the surprises: the soft *j*, *i* that sounds like 'ee', *w* which is **double v** in French, the name for *y* which means Greek 'i'.
- Fix your lower-case letter cards on the wall or board as shown below.

  a b c d e f g        h i j k l m n o p

  q r s t u v         w x y z

- Play the 'Song: *L'alphabet français*' from the CD-ROM two or three times, pointing to the letters as the children listen, then play it again, asking the children to join in.

### Vocabulary extension

- Look at a particular word, for example, *janvier*. Ask: '*A', c'est une consonne ou une voyelle ?* Do the same with *i* and *e*. Now with *j*: '*J', c'est une voyelle ou une consonne ?* Repeat with *n* and *v*. Practise the new words (**voyelle** and **consonne**).
- Look at a name or a word with an initial capital letter and ask, for example: *C'est un 'b' minuscule ou un 'B' majuscule ?* Discuss the conventions of capital letters for names – the same in French and English – but also some anomalies, for example there are no capitals for the days of the week and months in French.

## Core activities

- Have the word cards showing days and months on display around the room or on the classroom board. Tell the children you are going to spell out a word in French. *Écoutez bien ! Je vais épeler un mot. Regardez les mots. C'est quel mot ?* Use gestures to make sure your meaning is clear.
- Ask the children to take their mini whiteboards (*Prenez les ardoises*). Tell them you are going to spell a word. They should listen and write (*Je vais épeler un mot. Écoutez bien et écrivez !*). Make sure they all show you their results at the same time by using *Un, deux, trois ... montrez-moi !* so that you can assess each child's progress.
- Give out copies of photocopiable page 38 (*Le graphisme*) which shows the alphabet written in a French handwriting style. Discuss the similarities with and differences from their own style of handwriting. Do they like the French style? Explain to them that handwriting is very important in French schools. Children spend a lot of time learning to make the shapes which make up letter forms in art lessons using different media. Children are expected to produce handwriting of a very high quality. Exercise books are often ruled out with many fine lines and squares to allow children to perfect the length and width of the letter shapes which make up their handwriting. Invite the children to create a decorative poster of their names in French handwriting style, embellished with pictures of their hobbies, homes and so on. You can see further examples of French handwriting in the 'Film: *L'École Jeanne d'Arc*' from the CD-ROM (Unit 3).

## Extension activities

- Challenge the pupils to spell some French words using 'Interactive activity: *Comment ça s'écrit ?*' from the CD-ROM.
- If the children have come across words containing accents, this would be a good opportunity to introduce this additional aspect of spelling in French. Teach the children to say *accent aigu, accent grave, accent circonflexe, c cédille*. In a similar way to the vocabulary extension activity above, point to accented letters in words and ask, for example: *C'est un accent aigu ou un accent grave ?* Use familiar words such as *éléphant, père , fenêtre, garçon*.

### Resources

Interactive flashcard:
*L'alphabet français*

Interactive activity:
*Comment ça s'écrit ?*

Photocopiable page 38:
*Le graphisme*

Photocopiable:
*L'alphabet français*

Song:
*L'alphabet français*

Film:
*L'École Jeanne d'Arc*

### Preparation

A set of alphabet cards

Home-made word cards showing days of the week (from Unit 3) and months

Mini whiteboards

Interactive whiteboard

# Unit 5: L'alphabet et le graphisme

## Tips

The Teachers' TV video at www.teachers.tv/video/24021 explains the place of handwriting in the French education system.

## Cross-curricular ideas

**PE: To carry out warm-up activities in French.**

Sing the alphabet in French as a warm-up using the well-known American Marines marching chant. Ask the children to march rhythmically behind you in the hall or gym. Establish the marching before you start to sing. The children should repeat the lines as you sing:

A B C D E F G (A B C D E F G)       H I J K L M N (H I J K L M N)
O P Q R S T U (O P Q R S T U)       V W X Y Z (V W X Y Z)

Once the children have grasped this idea you could use the spelling of a person's name or the name of your town. Call out a letter for every four steps taken. Everyone should call out the name or word once your spelling is finished. Vary the atmosphere by marching very quietly and speaking or singing quietly. Marines are disciplined, remember!

## Five-minute follow-ups

- Play 'Hangman' (*le pendu*): think of a familiar word and draw a series of dashes on the board, each representing a letter. The children must guess the word by suggesting letters in French. With each failed attempt the teacher draws a new element of the 'gallows' and hanged man.

- Choose helpers by spelling their names in French. Preface with *Écoutez bien la classe. Je choisis quelqu'un pour m'aider* (Listen carefully, class. I am choosing someone to help me).

---

## Key words

### Core:

*l'alphabet* (m) – the alphabet
*une lettre* – a letter
*un mot* – a word
*le jour* – the day
*le mois* – the month
*janvier* – January
*février* – February
*mars* – March
*avril* – April
*mai* – May
*juin* – June
*juillet* – July
*août* – August
*septembre* – September
*octobre* – October
*novembre* – November
*décembre* – December
*une ardoise* – a mini whiteboard (literally = a slate)
*le graphisme* – the handwriting

### Extension:

*une voyelle* – a vowel
*une consonne* – a consonant
*b minuscule* – lower-case b
*B majuscule* – upper-case B
*un accent aigu* – an acute accent (as in *éléphant*)
*un accent grave* – a grave accent (as in *père*)
*un circonflexe* – a circumflex (as in *fenêtre*)
*une c cédille* – a c cedilla (as in *garçon*)

## Language points

- Teachers should not underestimate the importance of making phoneme/grapheme links explicit to the children. When you introduce new word cards, ask the children to look for patterns. For example, look for words with an 'ee' sound as in *petit* (letter *i*). Ask them routinely to look for surprises (*Est-ce qu'il y a des surprises ?*) such as a silent letter *h* or a silent terminal *s*.

## Key phrases

### Core:

*Voici l'alphabet français* – That's the French alphabet

*Prenez les ardoises* – Take your whiteboards

*Écoutez bien et écrivez* – Listen carefully and write

*Épelez ...* – Spell...

*votre prénom* – your first name

*votre nom de famille* – your family name

# Unit 6: J'adore mon uniforme !

## Resources

Interactive flashcard:
*Mon uniforme scolaire*

Interactive activity:
*Un, une ou des ?*

Photocopiable page 39:
*Les dominos*

Film:
*L'École Jeanne D'Arc*

## Objectives

**To learn the vocabulary for clothes; to express and give reasons for preferences.**

## Introducing the vocabulary

- Introduce items of school clothing using 'Interactive flashcard: *Mon uniforme scolaire*' from the CD-ROM. Click on singular items first, then plural ones. Use a range of repetition techniques to reinforce vocabulary (see Introduction and Tips opposite).

- Explain to the children that you are going to give them one minute to memorise the words but first they have two minutes to discuss their strategies for learning the words as a group. Before they do this, listen to the words once more. After the two minutes are up, give the children one minute to write their list on their whiteboard or say the items to each other. Before clicking on the items again, elicit answers from each group. Ask the successful groups to share their strategies.

- For those who didn't remember, try to unpick what the problem was with their strategy. Focus on the language: which words are easier/more difficult to remember and why? Which words surprise them (for example, *un pantalon* – singular not plural)?

- Let the children complete 'Interactive activity: *Un, une ou des ?*' from the CD-ROM to reinforce the use of the correct article.

## Preparation

Mini whiteboards

Illustrations of your own designs for a new school uniform, ready to present on the interactive whiteboard

French-English dictionaries

Two bags of mixed clothes

Interactive whiteboard

## Core activities

- Introduce the phrase *Pour aller à l'école je mets ...* then use it to play a 'Granny went to market' style game. Begin by drawing an item on a whiteboard then use the item to complete the sentence eg *Pour aller à l'école je mets un pantalon.* Pass the whiteboard on to the first child who should draw an item of their choice on the whiteboard, add it to the sentence then pass the whiteboard on. When the children understand how to play the game, let them play it in groups.

- If the children have prior knowledge of other clothes and places they could make new sentence stems such as *Pour aller à la plage je mets ...*, with other children finishing the sentence. For less confident children this could be done the other way around, so you say *un maillot de bain* and the children say *la plage.*

- Discuss the fact that children in French schools don't wear uniform. Watch the 'Film: *L'École Jeanne d'Arc*' from the CD-ROM (unit 3) to see what children wear. Do they think that not wearing a uniform is a good or a bad thing?

## Extension activities

- Ask the children what a French schoolchild might say about what they put on in the morning. Introduce the phrases, *Je n'ai pas d'uniforme; je mets ce que je veux !* ( I don't have a uniform; I wear what I like!)

- Teach or revise the extension phrases (eg *c'est moche*) and encourage the children to use the phrases to say how they feel about their school uniform (if they have one). Then tell them that you have devised a fabulous new uniform for the school. Present your picture on the interactive whiteboard using slow reveal/spotlight functions. At each point, elicit the children's reaction to your designs.

- The children could then design their own uniforms and label them in French. This could be used as an opportunity to teach the children how to use a bilingual dictionary to extend their writing. Together show them how to look up a new item of clothing and ask the children whether the word is masculine or feminine. Ask them to explain how they know.

# Unit 6: J'adore mon uniforme !

## Cross-curricular ideas

**Literacy: To explore a situation through drama.**

Tell the children to imagine that they are going to a friend's party. They should work in pairs to act out a role-play situation – one child is trying to persuade the other to wear particular clothes using phrases such as *Mets un t-shirt* and so on.

**PSHE: To discuss the role of school uniforms.**

Hold a class discussion, in English, about the role of the school uniform. What is its purpose? What are the advantages of a uniform? What are the disadvantages? How do they feel about their own school uniform? How could it be improved?

## Five-minute follow-ups

○ Divide the class into two teams and bring out the two bags of clothes. Ask a volunteer from each team to come to the front. Say *je mets ...* (plus item of clothing). The first person to find and put on the correct item of clothing wins a point for their team.

○ Children can practise the vocabulary from this unit with photocopiable page 39 (*Les dominos*). In this version of Dominoes, the children should match up pictures with corresponding sentences. Each child in a group of three should cut out a set of dominoes to make a playing set of 30.

## Tips

When introducing vocabulary, ask the children to repeat the words in a happy/ sad style or using the voices of famous people or characters. Try chanting the words and saying the words faster and faster then quieter and quieter and so on. Another useful technique is to ask the children to guess words that you mouth silently.

## Key words

### Core:

*un polo* – a polo shirt
*un gilet* – a cardigan
*une jupe* – a skirt
*des collants* (m) – tights
*des chaussettes* (f) – socks
*un sweat* – a sweatshirt
*un pantalon* – trousers
*des chaussures* (f) – shoes
*un maillot de bain* – a swimming costume

### Extension:

*avec* – with
*parce que* – because
*rouge* – red
*orange* – orange
*rose* – pink
*jaune* – yellow
*marron* – brown
*bleu(e)* – blue
*blanc(he)* – white
*vert(e)* – green
*noir(e)* – black
*gris(e)* – grey

## Key phrases

### Core:

*mon uniforme scolaire* – my school uniform
*Pour aller à l'école je mets ...* – For school I put on/I wear...

### Extension:

*Je n'ai pas d'uniforme* – I don't have a uniform
*Je mets ce que je veux !* – I wear what I like!
*j'adore* – I love
*je déteste* – I hate

*je préfère* – I prefer
*j'aime* – I like/love
*c'est laid* – it's ugly
*c'est moche* – it's ugly/horrible
*c'est beau* (m) – beautiful
*c'est belle* (f) – beautiful
*c'est super* – great

Note that **super** can also be used to emphasise either positive or negative adjectives, for example **super moche** (really ugly), **super beau** (really **beautiful**).

## Language points

○ The children may need some help to realise that the gender of the item of clothing bears no relation to the gender of the wearer.

○ If the children already know colours you could encourage them to put them together with the new vocabulary from this unit. If you wish to avoid the issue of adjectival agreement at this stage, use only colours such as *rouge*, *orange*, *rose* and *jaune* which can be used with both masculine and feminine nouns in the singular (an *s* would be added to the plural form but this doesn't affect the pronunciation).

# Unit 7: Dans ma salle de classe

## Objectives

**To learn the vocabulary for classroom furniture and objects; to learn simple prepositions.**

## Introducing the vocabulary

- Use 'Interactive flashcard: *Dans ma salle de classe*' from the CD-ROM to introduce items of classroom furniture a few at a time. Start with *la table*, a cognate. Teach *un* words and *une* words separately to reinforce differentiated pronunciation.
- Play *Montrez-moi*. You say an object and the children have to point to it, for example: *Montrez-moi la porte ! Montrez-moi la chaise !* Develop this into a game of *Jacques a dit* (see Unit 1).

### Vocabulary extension

- Introduce other classroom items, incidentally, as you use them.

## Core activities

- Show the children the large word cards made from the photocopiable page from the CD-ROM. Introduce '*le tableau blanc*' and use the blank boxes to add any new words you have introduced. Practise reading the words aloud. Have fun with exaggerated pronunciation. Play 'Secret signal' and 'Hot/cold' (see Introduction) to give further pronunciation practice.
- Discuss surprises in the spellings. There are a lot here: the *sh* sound of *chaise*, the *o* sound of *-eau* in *tableau*, the *t* sound of *th* in *bibliothèque*, the French *r* sound in *fenêtre* and *ordinateur*, the silent *s* at the end of *tapis*.
- Invite the children to create their own labels by writing the words from memory and sticking them to the correct objects in the classroom. Alternatively, the children could complete 'Interactive activity: *Dans ma salle de classe*' from the CD-ROM and label the items in the picture.
- Use 'Interactive flashcard: *Où est le lapin ?*' from the CD-ROM to introduce prepositions. You may wish to introduce them gradually, say two at a time. You could also introduce or practise prepositions using a soft toy or puppet and a cardboard box. Position the toy somewhere in relation to the box and ask: *Où est* [name of toy] *? Sur la boîte ? Sous la boîte ?* and so on.
- Play guessing games. While the children are out at break, hide the toy, initially in and around the box, then around the classroom, so that the children start to combine the prepositions with classroom furniture language. You say: *Où est* [name of toy] *? Il/elle se cache* (he/she is hiding – use gesture to make meaning clear). *Où est-il/elle ?* The children should ask, and you should reply, with full sentences, for example: *Il/elle est derrière l'ordinateur ? Non, il/elle n'est pas derrière l'ordinateur.* Return to this game again and again, widening your range of prepositions and introducing more hiding places as the children learn more language.

## Extension activity

- Ask the children to play the guessing game in pairs by 'hiding' an imaginary teddy or toy. Encourage the 'seekers' to produce whole sentences when they guess, for example, *Il/elle est devant le tableau blanc ?* The 'hider' should reply with a full sentence *Il/elle n'est pas devant le tableau blanc* until the correct guess is made. The children will have heard you say these phrases in the whole-class activity. Just a little repetition at the start should give them the confidence to play the game with this extra challenge.

---

## Resources

Interactive flashcards:
*Dans ma salle de classe*
*Où est le lapin ?*

Interactive activity:
*Dans ma salle de classe*

Photocopiable page 40:
*Cache le lapin*

Photocopiable:
*Dans ma salle de classe*

## Preparation

A large set of cards made from 'Photocopiable: *Dans ma salle de classe*', colour coded for gender (eg red for feminine, blue for masculine)

A soft toy or puppet and a cardboard box

Interactive whiteboard

---

# Unit 7: Dans ma salle de classe

## Tips

Have a French teddy or puppet in your classroom. Bring it out when French is being taught or spoken. Younger children will find it reassuring, while older children will enjoy the opportunity for role play.

## Cross-curricular ideas

**Maths: To play a game with grid coordinates.**

Give the children a copy each of photocopiable page 40 (*Cache le lapin*). The children should use the grid with coordinates to take turns to hide and guess the hiding place of the rabbit.

**PSHE and citizenship: To exchange information with a school in a French-speaking country.**

Make a link with a French-speaking school and create a video link to see inside each other's classrooms. See www.etwinning.net/en/pub/index.htm or www.britishcouncil.org/etwinning.htm

## Five-minute follow-ups

- Once you have your labels in place on the classroom furniture, play 'Hangman' (*le pendu*) with the new words (see Unit 5: Five-minute follow-ups).
- Use the new language whenever you can in the natural classroom context. Dramatically 'mislay' something – your glasses (*mes lunettes*), your pencil case (*ma trousse*) or your bag (*mon sac*) – and tell the children, for example: *Oh, j'ai perdu mes lunettes. Où sont mes lunettes ? J'ai perdu ma trousse. Où est ma trousse ?* Get the children to suggest where your lost property might be until you find it again.

---

### Key words

**Core:**

*la table* – the table
*la chaise* – the chair
*la porte* – the door
*la fenêtre* – the window
*la poubelle* – the bin
*la bibliothèque* – the bookcase
*le tapis* – the carpet/mat
*le placard* – the cupboard
*l'ordinateur* (m) – the computer
*le tableau blanc* – the whiteboard
*la salle de classe* – the classroom
*un chapeau* – a hat
*un lapin* – a rabbit
*sur* – on
*sous* – under
*dans* – in
*devant* – in front (of)
*derrière* – behind
*la boîte* – the box
*le nounours* – the teddy
*la peluche* – the soft toy
*le pantin* – the puppet

### Key phrases

**Core:**

*Bonne nuit !* – Goodnight!
*Où est (-il) ?* – Where is (he)?
*Montrez-moi !* – Show me!
*Cache le lapin* – Hide the rabbit

**Extension:**

*Il est* – He/it is
*Elle est* – She/it is
*Il n'est pas* – He/it is not
*Elle n'est pas* – She/it is not
*J'ai perdu ...* – I've lost ...
*mes lunettes* – my glasses
*ma trousse* – my pencil case
*mon sac* – my bag

### Language points

This unit provides a natural context for children to use the definite article ('the' in English) – *le* (masculine), *la* (feminine), *les* (plural). They also encounter *l'* in *l'ordinateur*, a masculine word. Irrespective of gender, *l'* is used with singular nouns which begin with a vowel or a silent *h* (*l'avion, l'eau, l'usine, l'idée, l'orange, l'hôtel, l'hôpital, l'hélicoptère*).

# Unit 8: Maths, les maths !

## Objectives

**To revise subject vocabulary; to listen to a song for meaning and identify rhyme.**

## Introducing the vocabulary

- This unit builds on Unit 3: *Ma matière préferée* so begin by revising the subject vocabulary from this unit. Ask the children what school subjects they can remember. Put their suggestions on the whiteboard and number each suggestion.

- Play the 'Song: *Maths, les maths*' from the CD-ROM. (Do not give the children copies of the song transcript or translation at this point.) Ask the children to write the numbers of any of the school subjects they hear on their whiteboards.

- Give out the phrase cards. Ask the children to turn over the cards on their desk. Tell them that they should hold up the card when they hear their phrase in the song. Play the song again.

- Play the first verse of the song once more. The children on the tables with the two half sentences from this verse (**Sophie**) should stand up. Ask the children which part of the sentence is first, drawing their attention to the rhyme. Then ask the children on the other tables to work out who they are paired with. This could be done as a human sentence activity with children coming out to the front to make complete sentences.

- The activity on photocopiable page 41 (*Qu'est-ce qu'ils aiment faire ?*) will give the children an opportunity to apply the phrases they have learned in a writing task. The activity will be differentiated by outcome so the children's sentences may range from simple repetitive sentences (*Manon aime écouter la musique. Manon aime l'anglais. Manon n'aime pas le chocolat.*) to more complex sentences which use pronouns and connectives (*Manon aime l'anglais. Elle aime aussi écouter la musique mais elle n'aime pas le chocolat.*).

## Core activities

- Open the transcript of the song on 'Photocopiable: *Maths, les maths 2*' and ask the children to read the words as they listen to the song. Then elicit the meaning of the sentences from the children. Decide on an appropriate mime for each section of the song.

- Say some of the sentences in order to practise the actions. Listen to the song again, this time inviting the children to do the agreed actions; they could do this in groups or pairs with one pupil doing one half of the sentence and the other doing the other part.

- Say a sentence from the song (eg **Elle dessine.**). Can the children remember the name of the person who would say the sentence?

- Mime a sentence for the class and give points to the tables which make the best sentence.

- Ask the children to create a stop-frame animation of the song. They should work through the song, saying each line and doing the actions. After a while say 'stop' and ask some groups to show the action for the line they are on. The rest of the class have to guess what the sentence is.

- When the children are very familiar with the song, ask them to complete the interactive activities from the CD-ROM where they have to decide which sentences are true and which are false.

---

### Resources

Interactive activities:
*C'est qui ? 1*
*C'est qui ? 2*

Photocopiable page 41:
*Qu'est-ce qu'ils aiment faire ?*

Photocopiables:
*Maths, les maths 1*
*Maths, les maths 2*

Song:
*Maths, les maths*

Translation:
*Maths, les maths*

### Preparation

Mini whiteboards

Phrase cards made from 'Photocopiable: *Maths, les maths 1*', divided between groups and placed face down on the tables before the beginning of the class.

Pictures of children from magazines, enough for one per pair

Interactive whiteboard

## Tips

Keep a list of all names on a French name board. These can then be used if pupils need to choose a French name for any role plays.

## Extension activity

- This activity involves building up a profile of imaginary children in the style of the game 'Consequences'. Begin by discussing French names and write a list of the names that the children know on the board. Hand out the magazine pictures and explain to the class that they are going to build up profiles of the children in the pictures. Ask the children to stick the picture at the top of a piece of paper and write the person's name underneath. They should then pass the paper on to the next pair, who write *il/elle aime ...* (plus school subject). The next pair should write what the person doesn't like (*il/elle n'aime pas ...*) and the final pair should write what he or she prefers (*il/elle préfère ...*). These profiles could then be used as a basis for hot-seating, with pupils asking questions such as *Tu aimes les maths ?*

## Cross-curricular ideas

**Music: To compose a new tune for a song.**

Challenge the children to write their own tune for the song *Maths, les maths*. They could do it in a different style such as calypso, rock and roll or even in the style of Mozart.

**Art and design: To make a collage to illustrate a song.**

Divide up the lines of the song between groups and ask the children to create a collage of their line. Arrange the collages along a wall or corridor with the lines of the song for an eye-catching display.

## Five-minute follow-ups

- Practise singing or saying the song in different styles and moods – quickly, slowly, sadly, excitedly and so on.
- Use phrases from the song with the wrong ending and challenge the children to correct you. More experienced or confident children may be able to invent their own endings for others to correct.

---

### Key words

**Core:**

*le français* – French
*le déjeuner* – lunch
*l'anglais* (m) – English
*l'histoire* (f) – history
*la géo(graphie)* – geography
*les maths* (f pl) – maths
*facile* – easy
*difficile* – difficult
*mais* – but
*manger* – to eat
*boire* – to drink
*une glace* – an ice cream
*le chocolat* – chocolate

### Key phrases

**Core:**

*c'est difficile* – it's difficult
*(le français) est bien facile* – (French) is quite easy
*il/elle aime* – he/she likes
*il/elle dessine* – he/she draws
*il/elle n'aime pas* – he/she doesn't like
*il/elle préfère* – he/she prefers
*il/elle écrit* – he/she writes
*il/elle écoute des disques* – he/she listens to discs
*en classe* – in school

**Extension:**

*Tu aimes (les maths) ?* – Do you like maths?

### Language points

In this unit the children are introduced to some more verbs in the third person singular. At this point there is no need to explore verb conjugations but, for some pupils, teachers may find it appropriate to highlight the pattern of the *e* ending on the *–er* present tense verbs.

# Unit 9: Les règles de l'école

## Objectives

**To explore and express school rules; to practise using bilingual dictionaries.**

## Introducing the vocabulary

- This unit focuses on the children working out/finding out the meanings of words and phrases for themselves using context, previous knowledge and dictionaries.
- Show the children how to look words up in a bilingual dictionary; they may need help working out which half of the dictionary they need to use.
- Write the infinitive forms (*écouter*, *courir* etc) of the verbs listed in the key words onto the board. Give the children time to look up the meanings of these words in the dictionary, then ask them to see if they can group them. You may want to split the list or give some children fewer words.
- Check that the children have understood that the words they have looked up are all verbs. Ensure that they have found the meanings that are appropriate for the context of school rules. (Sometimes, as in English, verbs can have more than one meaning.)

### Vocabulary extension

- Some children may wish to look up other words which could be used to make sentences with the verbs.

## Core activities

- Using 'Interactive flashcard: *Le nouvel élève*' from the CD-ROM click on each picture in turn to tell the story. After each frame elicit from the children what is happening. Focus on the language for explaining rules. Can the children identify how to say: 'you have to' (*il faut*), 'you must not' (*il ne faut pas*) and 'you can' (*on peut*)?
- Ask the children to complete 'Interactive activity: *Les règles de l'école*' from the CD-ROM which involves matching sentence endings to the phrases *il faut, il ne faut pas* and *on peut*. The activity contains some new vocabulary so the children may need to use the dictionaries again. Remind them to use context to help them make educated guesses about meaning before looking a word up in the dictionary. After the activity discuss how successful the children's guesses were and discuss any surprises.
- Play a game to consolidate this language. You will need space for this activity. Take three sentences from the interactive activity or interactive flashcard. Write each sentence out and cut them up into individual words/phrases. Divide the class into three teams. As a relay race, each member of the team should run to the front and collect one word/phrase. When they have all the words for the first sentence the first team to make the sentence correctly wins a point. Repeat with the other two sentences.
- Put the correct sentences on the board and then set up a chant. For example, one half of the room says *il ne faut pas* and the other half chants back *manger en classe*. One pupil at the front could signal which of the sentence endings they should use.

## Extension activity

- Elicit from the children what they feel should happen next. They could either prepare a short sketch in groups or write their own cartoon-strip story about rules. They could begin by completing photocopiable page 42 (*Bienvenue aux scouts*), which might give them more ideas. Less confident children may prefer just to work through the photocopiable page. More confident children could add their own pictures and ideas to the photocopiable page. At the end of the session, invite the children to present their stories to each other.

---

### Resources

Interactive flashcard:
*Le nouvel élève*

Interactive activity:
*Les règles de l'école*

Photocopiable page 42:
*Bienvenue aux scouts*

### Preparation

Bilingual dictionaries

Three sentences from 'Interactive flashcard: *Le nouvel élève*' or 'Interactive activity: *Les règles de l'école*', written out and cut up into individual words (three sets of each sentence required)

Interactive whiteboard

# Unit 9: Les règles de l'école

## Tips

Phrases are more empowering for children than long lists of nouns. Make a 'phrase wall' where children can add their most useful phrases with one or two example endings.

## Cross-curricular ideas

**PSHE and citizenship: To take part in a discussion about rules and relationships.**

The context of this unit lends itself to a discussion both of school rules and their rationale and also to the feelings of new pupils and how best to help them. This discussion would need to happen in English but the children could then make up a 'welcome pack' in French and English for new pupils to their class/school.

**Music: To create a school song which incorporates their own school rules.**

Challenge the children to compose a piece of music which incorporates your school rules. They could create interesting effects by using French phrases then echoing them with their English equivalents.

## Five-minute follow-ups

- Try to use the phrases *il faut*, *il ne faut pas* and *on peut* throughout the school day. Encourage the pupils to use *on peut ... ?* (with rising intonation) themselves when asking permission and *il faut*, *il ne faut pas* when they see other children misbehaving!

## Key words

### Core:

*écouter* – to listen to
*courir* – to run
*manger* – to eat
*crier* – to shout
*respecter* – to respect
*jouer* – to play
*porter* – to wear
*aller* – to go
*être* – to be
*parler* – to speak
*Voici ...* – Here is...
*un (nouvel) élève* – a (new) pupil
*sourd(e)* – deaf
*gentil(le)* – kind
*fort(e)* – loud
*poli(e)* – polite
*donc* – so
*maintenant* – now
*le chewing-gum* – chewing gum
*les couloirs* (m)– the corridors
*la recré(ation)* – break/playtime
*un ballon* – a ball
*dur* – hard

### Extension:

*Bienvenue* – Welcome
*seulement* – only

## Key phrases

### Core:

*Ecoutez, les enfants* – Listen, children
*Assieds-toi là* – Sit there
*à côté de* – next to
*Tu peux (lui) expliquer les règles ?* – Can you explain the rules (to him/her)?
*Il faut (lever la main/respecter les autres élèves)* – You/one must (raise your hand/respect other pupils)

## Key phrases

*Il ne faut pas (crier/manger en classe)* – You/one mustn't (shout/eat in class)
*On peut (jouer au foot/aller aux toilettes)* – We/one can (play football/go to the toilet)
*s'il est nécessaire* – if it's necessary
*A toute à l'heure* – See you soon

### Extension:

*un groupe de scouts* – a scout group
*boire de la limonade/de l'eau* – to drink lemonade/water
*écouter de la musique* – to listen to music
*bonne idée* – good idea

## Language points

The phrases *il faut* and *on peut* need to be followed by the infinitive. You may need to explain this to pupils as the 'dictionary form' of the verb. A clue for pupils to check whether the words they are using are infinitives is that they must always end with either *–er*, *–ir* or *–re*.

# Unit 10: Quelle heure est-il ?

## Objective

**To learn to tell the time on the hour, half-hour, quarter to and quarter past.**

## Introducing the vocabulary

- Warm up by counting to 11. Play *'Onze'* in groups or as a class. The children stand up and count round the class in French. Each person can choose to say either one, two or three numbers, for example: the first child says *un, deux*, the second says *trois*, the third says *quatre, cinq, six* and so on. The child who has to say *onze* is out and has to sit down. The next child then begins from one again. Gradually all the children will be eliminated until only one winner remains.

- Open 'Interactive flashcard: *Quelle heure est-il ? 1*' from the CD-ROM. Click on and listen to the time shown on the first two clocks. Before clicking on the third, ask the children if they can guess what the time will be. Do the same with clocks four, five and six. Then say random times (on the hour only) and ask the children to draw or write the time on their mini whiteboards. Finally click on *midi* and *minuit* on the interactive flashcard and ask the children what the English equivalents are.

## Core activities

- Arrange the class into groups and ask one child in each group to write or draw a time on their whiteboard without showing the rest of the group. The others have to guess the time by asking a time, for example, *Il est huit heures ?* The first child should respond with *plus* (if their number is higher) or *moins* (if their number is lower).

- Open 'Interactive flashcard: *Quelle heure est-il ? 2*' from the CD-ROM and click on clocks one to three, which introduce the half-hour. The clocks in the pictures have a dummy to remind the children of the sound of the word *demie*.

- Practise the half-hour times in a 'total physical response' style: find an action to represent each word, for example: *il* could be moving hand like an eel, *heure* could be face of disgust. Invite ideas for actions for each word from the children. When you have agreed what the actions will be, say a sentence at the same time as doing the actions and ask the children to copy the actions. Then say a sentence and ask the children to do the actions and repeat the words. Finally, just do the actions and challenge the children to work out the complete sentence.

- Go back to 'Interactive flashcard: *Quelle heure est-il ? 2*' from the CD-ROM. Tell the children that you want them to listen for the French word for 'quarter'. Click on clocks four to six. Discuss the spelling of the word *quart* and the links with the English word.

- Ask the children what they notice about the word order when telling the time in French. Then focus on quarter to. (Note that the clock has a sad face because the car has gone.)

- Play bingo using the cards from photocopiable page 43 (*Loto*). Give each child a card and then act as the caller. Use only times on the hour (including *midi* and *minuit*), half-hour, quarter past and quarter to. The game could be differentiated by asking children to work in pairs or asking them to listen for just one line on their card. When pupils are more confident with the language they could then do this in small groups with the most confident child/children acting as caller.

## Extension activities

- Stick three or four cards featuring the names of school subjects on the board. Elicit times for each lesson from the children and stick the relevant time cards next to the subjects. Arrange the cards in time order to create a visual timetable. You have two minutes to memorise the timetable. With your back to the board, one child says a time and you have to say the subject or vice versa. Play this a few times and then allow the children to play in pairs.

- Let the children complete 'Interactive activity: *C'est quel cours ?*' from the CD-ROM which asks further questions based on a school timetable.

### Resources

Interactive flashcards:
*Quelle heure est-il ? 1*
*Quelle heure est-il ? 2*

Interactive activity:
*C'est quel cours ?*

Photocopiable page 43:
*Loto*

### Preparation

Mini whiteboards

Teaching clock

Home-made cards with hour and half-hour times written on them

Home-made word cards featuring school subjects (see Unit 3 *'Ma matière préferée'*)

Interactive whiteboard

# Unit 10: Quelle heure est-il ?

## Tips

When telling the time in French, hours come before minutes. Ask the children to spot any other examples where French word order differs from English.

## Cross-curricular ideas

**PE: To play warm-up games following instructions in French.**

As a warm-up in PE, play *Quelle heure est-il Monsieur Loup ?* (What's the time Mr Wolf?). You could also try a variation on hopscotch, where the children write times in boxes instead of numbers.

**Geography: To explore time zones.**

Using a time-zone map, invite the children to say what the time is in different countries around the world. Say, for example, *Il est une heure en Angleterre, quelle heure est-il au Mexique ?* Use countries which are easy to recognise such as *Australie*, *Inde*, *Italie*, *Mexique*, *Grèce*, *Thaïlande*.

## Five-minute follow-ups

- French people often use the 24-hour clock in normal conversation, so once your pupils know their numbers up to 59 they can do the same! Word order in this form is the same as English, so 20.30 is *vingt heures trente*.

### Key words

**Core:**

*midi* – midday
*minuit* – midnight
*et* – and
*moins* – less
*plus* – more

### Key phrases

**Core:**

*Quelle heure est-il ?* – What time is it?
*Il est (une) heure* – It's one o'clock
*Il est (deux) heures* – It's two o'clock
*Il est (trois heures) et demie* – It's half past (three)
*Il est (quatre) heures et quart* – It's quarter past (four)
*Il est (cinq) moins le quart* – It's quarter to (five)

**Extension:**

*C'est quel cours ?* – Which lesson is it?
*C'est (les maths)* – It's (maths)
*Il est (deux heures) dix* – It's ten past (two)
*Il est (deux heures) moins dix* – It's ten to (two)
*Vingt heures trente* – 20.30

### Language points

- To say 'minutes past' in French you just say the number, for example, *trois heures vingt*, except for quarter past where you need *et* (*et quart*). Similarly times up to the hour are simply *moins* plus the number, for example, *quatre heures moins dix* except for quarter to (*moins le quart*). Note that *moins* usually means less so it is 'four o'clock less ten minutes', instead of 'ten minutes to four', as in English. Also note the word order. When telling the time in French, start with the hour rather than the minutes.

- The *x* of *deux*, *dix* and *six* is pronounced as a *z* before *heures*.

# Unit 11: Bienvenue à notre école

## Objective

**To describe their own school orally and in writing.**

## Introducing the vocabulary

- Use 'Interactive flashcard: *Notre école*' from the CD-ROM to show the different parts of the school. Click on the picture and ask the children to suggest what the words mean. Discuss the pronunciation of the words and ask the children if they can think of any good ways to remember how to pronounce them.
- Mouth the words silently and challenge the children to guess what they are.
- Choose one of the places in the school and clap the syllables. Can the children guess what the word is?
- Working in pairs, ask the children to choose three parts of the school they have been to today. Can they tell their partner where they've been using mime?
- Send the children off with Digiblue cameras to take funny photos of the school or ask them to take photos with a standard digital camera and use photo-editing software to create strange effects. Put all the pictures on a display board with the question: *Où suis-je ?* Other pupils should then write their guesses next to the photos.
- Ask the children to say what's in your school using the phrase: *Dans notre école il y a …*

## Core activities

- Use phrases from the Core phrases list below to describe a part of the school, for example: *Ici on mange*. Can the children guess the location? Try a few examples then ask the children to continue this activity in pairs or groups. You could extend this activity by incorporating some negative sentences (eg *Ici on ne mange pas*) or trying out some extended sentences (eg *J'aime cet endroit parce que je joue avec mes amis*).
- Ask the children to complete 'Interactive activity: *Qu'est-ce qu'on fait ?*' from the CD-ROM which will help to equip them with the language that they need for the main activity below.
- Explain to the children that they are going to make a presentation about their school; it could be a printed brochure, a video or a Powerpoint presentation. Before they begin, elicit from them words and phrases that they have learned throughout the units which they may wish to use.
- Give the children plenty of time to produce their presentations. Ideally the presentations should be used to introduce the school to a partner school in a French-speaking country or, if this isn't possible, to another local school where they are learning French. It could also be used to introduce the school to children who are coming up to the school from KS1 or as part of a transition project with a secondary school. Encourage the children to use language learned in other units, so they might say: *Voici notre salle de classe* ; *Il faut porter un uniforme* ; *On mange à midi*. Alternatively, they could start with a close-up of a pupil and use a voice-over, for example: *Voici Chloë. Elle mange.* They could then pan out to show the dining hall (*Elle est dans la cantine*) or there could be a twist (*Elle est dans la salle de classe ! Il ne faut pas manger dans la salle de classe !*).

## Extension activities

- You could use this as an opportunity for children to peer-review each others' work. Set them a specific target to look for such as correct spellings of places in school or accurate use of *le/la*.
- Invite the children to create their own ideal school using photocopiable page 44 (*Mon école idéale*).

## Cross-curricular ideas

**D&T: To design a model of an ideal school.**
Ask the children to work together to design a model of their ideal school. More confident children could write about this in French and add reasons for their choice of buildings and so on.

### Resources

Interactive flashcard:
*Notre école*

Interactive activity:
*Qu'est-ce qu'on fait ?*

Photocopiable page 44:
*Mon école idéale*

### Preparation

'Digiblue™' cameras or digital cameras/video cameras and photo/video-editing software, presentation software (such as Powerpoint®)

Interactive whiteboard

## Tips

Use the *on* form of the verb in classroom instructions, for example: *Allez, on écrit !* (Ok, let's write!)

**ICT: To use the internet to find information about schools in French-speaking countries.**

Challenge the children to use the internet to find out about school buildings in France or another French-speaking country. They could then make an interactive display of the information that they have found. The focus could be on similarities and differences.

**Art and Design: To make a book, poster or brochure about the school.**

As an extension to the core activity, invite the children to make a book, poster or brochure in French to tie in with the digital presentation. It could include information about the school, the pupils, their likes and dislikes, their uniform. The finished work could be displayed at parents' evening.

## Five-minute follow-ups

- Put labels in French around the whole school, colour-coded for masculine and feminine nouns. Go round and swap some of them periodically and award house points to the first pupils to come and tell you which labels are in the wrong place.

### Key words

**Core:**

*voici* – here is

*la cour* – playground

*la salle de classe* – classroom

*la salle des profs* – staffroom

*la cantine* – dining room

*le gymnase* – gym

*le terrain de sport* – sports field

*le centre de documentation et information (CDI)* – library (usually with computer facilities)

*la réception* – reception

*la bibliothèque* – library

*notre* – our

*ici* – here

**Extension:**

*cet endroit* – this place

*un instituteur* – male primary schoolteacher

*une institutrice* – female primary schoolteacher

*les poèmes* (m) – poems

*les devoirs* (m) – homework

*la nourriture* – food

*un skatepark* – a skatepark

*une piste de ski* – a ski slope

*une piscine* – a swimming pool

*des toilettes de luxe* (f) – luxury toilets

*une cabane dans les arbres* – a tree house

*un terrain de golf* – a golf course

*une fontaine de chocolat* – a chocolate fountain

*un trampoline* – a trampoline

*un fauteuil* – an armchair

### Key phrases

**Core:**

*miam-miam !* – yum-yum!

*où suis-je ?* – where am I?

*dans notre école* – in our school

*il y a* – there is/are

*on écrit* – we write

*on joue* – we play

*on mange* – we eat

*on écoute* – we listen to

*on fait* – we make/do

*on dessine* – we draw

*on boit* – we drink

*on ne (mange) pas* – we do not (eat)

*mes amis* – my friends

**Extension:**

*mon école idéale* – my ideal school

### Language points

- In Unit 8 the children were introduced to the *il/elle* form of some verbs. In this unit, we are using the same verb ending but with *on* eg *on écrit* (we write). *On* can mean 'one' but is much more commonly used to mean 'we'. It can be made negative by putting *ne* and *pas* around the verb eg *on ne mange pas* (we don't eat).

# Unit 12: Jeux pour la récréation

## Objective

**To learn, perform and enjoy finger and action rhymes, action songs, clapping games and a simple dance.**

## Introducing the vocabulary

- This unit focuses on learning action rhymes and songs and the vocabulary is introduced through the core activities, as the children encounter the rhymes. However, you may want to revise body parts (see Key words) before you begin as these appear in several of the songs.

- Introduce a few words at a time, asking the children to just listen (*écoutez*) to start with then to touch each body part (eg *touchez la tête*).

## Core activities

- Open 'Interactive flashcard: *Jeux pour la récréation 1*' from the CD-ROM and play the first action rhyme *Tourne, tourne, petit moulin*. Invite the children to guess the meaning of the first verse, using the pictures to help them (Turn little windmill, clap little hands, fly little bird, swim little fish).

- Next say each line with an appropriate action, for example: fists rotating round each other, clapping in rhythm, hands linked at the thumbs to imitate flying, then making a swimming motion. Ask the children to make the actions while you say the rhyme. Then invite them to repeat each line after you. Add the actions when the children are ready.

- Introduce verse two of *Tourne, tourne, petit moulin*. This verse is almost the same, but the verbs are in the past, so the windmill has turned, the bird has flown and so on.

- Use the same approach to introduce the other action rhymes on 'Interactive flashcard: *Jeux pour la récréation*' and *3* from the CD-ROM. For *Deux petits bonshommes* the actions are as follows: raise thumbs on each hand; touch thumbs; index fingers touch; middle fingers touch; ring fingers touch; little fingers touch; hands join to make a 'house'. The actions for '*Je cache mes yeux*' are shown in the interactive flashcard illustrations.

- When the children are familiar with the verses, challenge them to complete 'Interactive activity: *Jeux pour la récréation*' from the CD-ROM. The task involves putting the lines of some of the verses into the correct order.

- Open 'Interactive flashcard: *Le fermier dans son pré*' from the CD-ROM. *Le fermier dans son pré* is the French equivalent of 'The Farmer's in his Den' and uses the same tune. Ask the children to listen carefully as you sing a verse. Do they recognise the tune? Keep singing. Do they think the song has the same story as well as the same tune in both French and English? (They may pick out the word *fermier* and guess its meaning.) Get the children to suggest a gesture or pose for each character as you introduce them. Teach the song by saying or singing a line and asking the children to repeat until they are able to join in with you.

- Try out the songs on photocopiable page 45 (*Chansons et jeux pour la récréation*): *Le gouzi-gouzi* ('The Hokey-Cokey') and the traditional French song *La danse du Limousin*.

## Extension activities

- The children may notice that there is more than one way of writing 'small' in French. Can they guess why we write *petites mains*, but *petit poisson/oiseau/moulin*? The general rule in French is that adjectives 'agree' with the nouns they describe. So, in the *petites mains* example above an *s* is added to make both adjective and noun plural. Because *main* is a feminine word an *e* is also added.

- Use the rhymes *Deux petits bonshommes* and *Je cache mes yeux* to work on phoneme/grapheme links in French. Once the children have listened to and practised saying the rhyme, say the rhyme again, but ask them to touch their noses when they hear, for example, the sound *on* (õ). Get them to identify which letters make this sound. Try the same with the sound *oi* (wa). Get them to look for words which contain or end with silent letters. In *Je cache ...* they will meet the *on* sound again, as well as a silent *x*.

Interactive flashcard:
*Jeux pour la récréation 1*
*Jeux pour la récréation 2*
*Jeux pour la récréation 3*
*Le fermier dans son pré*

Interactive activity:
*Jeux pour la récréation*

Photocopiable page 45:
*Chansons et jeux pour la récréation*

Translation: *Chansons pour la récréation*

## Preparation

Interactive whiteboard

# Unit 12: Jeux pour la récréation

## Cross-curricular ideas

**PE/dance: To dance to French songs as part of a warm-up activity.**

Use the more energetic songs such as *La Danse du Limousin* and *Le Gouzi-Gouzi* for warm-up activities in PE or dance lessons.

**Literacy: To compare French songs and rhymes with similar ones in English.**

Look at the English versions of 'The Hokey-Cokey' and 'The Farmer's in his Den' and compare them with their French equivalents. Discuss similarities and differences. *Why might the cheese be significant in the French version of 'The Farmer's in his Den'?* Explain that the French are very fond of and proud of their cheeses. You could show the children photos of some hard cheeses, such as the large, round, hard cheeses found in the Pyrenees and the Jura, and maybe even try some!

## Five-minute follow-ups

- Make a mobile or poster of words that contain the sounds you focused on through these rhymes and songs. Add to your poster as you discover new ones.

### Tips

Although some of these rhymes may seem young for older primary-age children, they may like to perform them for or teach them to the KS1 children. You could also use the songs as part of a performance for parents or in an assembly.

If you have a link with a school in France or in a French-speaking country, make a collection of similar songs and rhymes in English. Put them into a book but also record the children performing the songs and send to your partner school.

Find new rhymes and songs on this French website: www.momes.net/comptines/comptines-chansons.html

### Key words

#### Core:

*les yeux* (m pl) – the eyes
*la main* – the hand
*le dos* – the back
*la tête* – the head
*l'épaule* (f) – the shoulder
*le pied* – the foot
*la hanche* – the hip
*la cheville* – the ankle
*le derrière* – the bottom
*gauche* – left
*droite* – right
*cache/cachez* – hide
*frappe/frappez* – clap
*lève/levez* – raise
*tourne/tournez* – turn
*vole/volez* – fly
*nage/nagez* – swim
*un moulin* – a windmill
*un oiseau* – a bird
*un poisson* – a fish
*une pomme* – an apple

*une noix* – a nut
*un champignon* – a mushroom
*un marron* – a chestnut
*le fermier* – the farmer
*le pré* – the meadow
*la femme* – the woman/wife
*l'enfant* – the child
*la nourrice* – the nursemaid
*le chat* – the cat
*la souris* – the mouse
*le fromage* – the cheese

### Key phrases

#### Core:

*en l'air* – in the air
*par terre* – on the ground
*gouzi-gouzi* – tickle, tickle / hokey-cokey

### Language points

- It is not necessary for the children to understand every word of each rhyme or song. They will grasp the gist quite easily.

# Jacques a dit

regardez

taisez-vous

écoutez bien

baissez la main

levez la main

ouvrez les yeux

fermez les yeux

asseyez-vous

levez-vous

touchez la table

**SCHOLASTIC** Photocopiable
www.scholastic.co.uk

# Mon cartable

J'aime aller à l'école

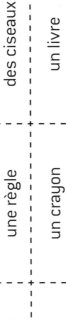
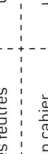
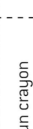

L'anglais

| une trousse | des ciseaux | une règle | des feutres | une calculette | un bic |
| | un livre | un crayon | un cahier | un taille crayon | une gomme |

**SCHOLASTIC** Photocopiable
www.scholastic.co.uk

Everyday French  À l'école

Prénom:

# Mon emploi du temps

| | le matin | | l'après-midi | |
|---|---|---|---|---|
| **lundi** | | | | |
| **mardi** | | | | |
| **mercredi** | | | | |
| **jeudi** | | | | |
| **vendredi** | | | | |

la récréation — le déjeuner

l'anglais (English)  la musique  les sciences (science)  le sport (PE)  l'informatique (ICT)

le français (French)  les maths  la géographie  l'histoire  le dessin (art)

# Coloriez les formes

- Coloriez ... les triangles en vert, les rectangles en brun, les hexagones en bleu, les carrés en rouge et les cercles en jaune.
- Découpez trois carrés, trois triangles et deux cercles. Faites-en une voiture ... !
- Découpez toutes les formes. Faites-en un train ? Une maison ? Une personne ?

# Le graphisme

- Ecris ton prénom à la manière française.
- Write your name in a French handwriting style.

*Aa*  *Bb*  *Cc*  *Dd*  *Ee*

*Ff*  *Gg*  *Hh*  *Ii*  *Jj*

*Kk*  *Ll*  *Mm*  *Nn*  *Oo*

*Pp*  *Qq*  *Rr*  *Ss*  *Tt*

*Uu*  *Vv*  *Ww*

*Xx*  *Yy*  *Zz*

# Les dominos

Cut out the dominoes and play with two other people.

| | |
|---|---|
|  | J'aime mon uniforme scolaire. |
|  | J'adore mes chaussures. |
|  | Je n'aime pas mon pantalon. |
|  | Je mets des chaussettes. |
|  | Je mets des collants. |
|  | Je mets des chaussures. |
|  | Je déteste ma jupe. |
|  | Je mets un gilet. |
|  | Je déteste mon uniforme scolaire. |
|  | J'adore mon polo. |

Illustration © Anna Godwin / Beehive Illustration

# Cache le lapin !

- You need a partner for this game. Sit opposite each other.
- Carefully cut out the rabbit opposite. Decide where you are going to 'hide' him and place your rabbit on the grid below. For example, if you choose to hide him 'dans le placard', place him in grid 2C. Make sure you keep your rabbit and grid hidden from your partner.
- Now take turns to guess. You might say, for example, 'Il est dans le placard'.
- The first one to guess correctly wins.

| | **1**<br>**la table** | **2**<br>**le placard** | **3**<br>**la porte** | **4**<br>**la poubelle** | **5**<br>**l'ordinateur** |
|---|---|---|---|---|---|
| **A**<br>**sur** | | | | | |
| **B**<br>**sous** | | | | | |
| **C**<br>**dans** | | | | | |
| **D**<br>**devant** | | | | | |
| **E**<br>**derrière** | | | | | |

Photocopiable

# Qu'est-ce qu'ils aiment faire ?

Use the pictures to help you write some sentences about the children.

**Théo**

_____

_____

_____

**Chloë**

_____

_____

_____

**Hugo**

_____

_____

_____

**Manon**

_____

_____

_____

_Illustration © Anna Godwin / Beehive Illustration_

# Bienvenue aux scouts

Cut out the lines of dialogue, below. Stick them onto the speech bubbles in the correct place.

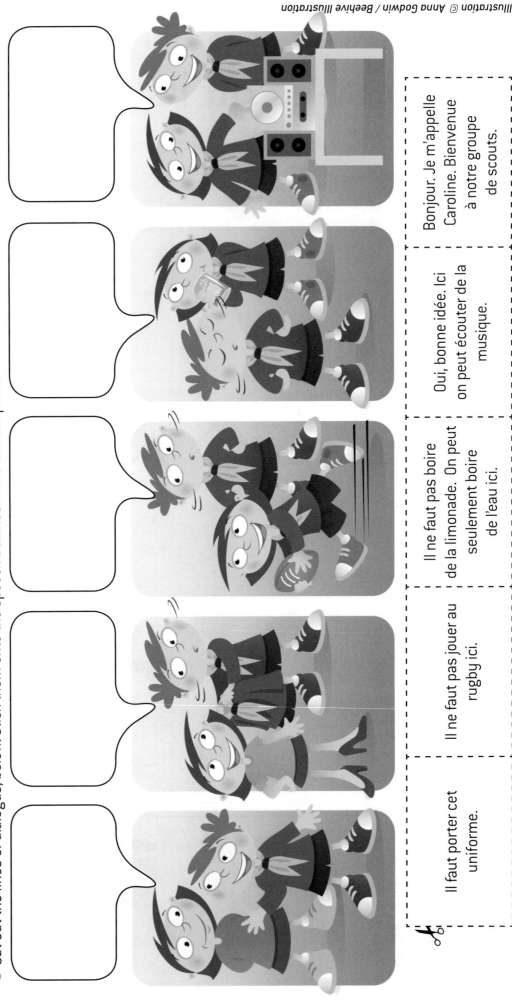

Illustration © Anna Godwin / Beehive Illustration

Bonjour. Je m'appelle Caroline. Bienvenue à notre groupe de scouts.

Oui, bonne idée. Ici on peut écouter de la musique.

Il ne faut pas boire de la limonade. On peut seulement boire de l'eau ici.

Il ne faut pas jouer au rugby ici.

Il faut porter cet uniforme.

# Loto

| | | | |
|---|---|---|---|
| 3.00 | 7.00 | 10.00 | 12.00 |
| 6.15 | 9.30 | 11.15 | 8.15 |
| 5.30 | 8.45 | 1.45 | 2.30 |

| | | | |
|---|---|---|---|
| 2.00 | 3.00 | 10.00 | 12.00 |
| 1.15 | 9.30 | 11.15 | 8.15 |
| 5.30 | 8.45 | 6.45 | 4.30 |

| | | | |
|---|---|---|---|
| 2.00 | 5.00 | 8.00 | 11.00 |
| 3.15 | 6.30 | 10.15 | 8.15 |
| 9.30 | 7.45 | 4.45 | 5.30 |

| | | | |
|---|---|---|---|
| 3.00 | 6.00 | 7.00 | 12.00 |
| 6.15 | 2.30 | 9.15 | 8.15 |
| 3.30 | 8.45 | 4.45 | 5.30 |

| | | | |
|---|---|---|---|
| 1.00 | 9.00 | 11.00 | 12.00 |
| 7.15 | 3.30 | 11.15 | 5.15 |
| 4.30 | 10.45 | 2.45 | 6.30 |

| | | | |
|---|---|---|---|
| 1.00 | 2.00 | 10.00 | 12.00 |
| 6.15 | 4.30 | 7.15 | 8.15 |
| 9.30 | 5.45 | 1.45 | 3.30 |

| | | | |
|---|---|---|---|
| 3.00 | 4.00 | 8.00 | 11.00 |
| 6.15 | 7.30 | 9.15 | 2.15 |
| 5.30 | 1.45 | 10.45 | 3.30 |

| | | | |
|---|---|---|---|
| 3.00 | 5.00 | 7.00 | 11.00 |
| 7.15 | 4.30 | 11.15 | 8.15 |
| 2.30 | 6.45 | 1.45 | 1.30 |

| | | | |
|---|---|---|---|
| 3.00 | 4.00 | 10.00 | 12.00 |
| 6.15 | 2.30 | 11.15 | 8.15 |
| 1.30 | 8.45 | 4.45 | 3.30 |

| | | | |
|---|---|---|---|
| 3.00 | 2.00 | 11.00 | 7.00 |
| 1.15 | 3.30 | 9.15 | 4.15 |
| 4.30 | 6.45 | 1.45 | 6.30 |

# Mon école idéale

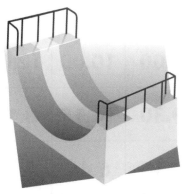

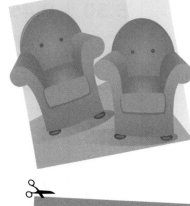

une piste de ski

un skatepark

une fontaine à chocolat

des fauteuils

des toilettes de luxe

une cabane dans les arbres

et il n'y a pas d'instituteurs !

un trampoline énorme

une piscine

un terrain de golf

une cour de récréation pour les garçons et une cour de récréation pour les filles

# Chansons et jeux pour la récréation

- This song is the French version of 'The Hokey-Cokey' and is sung to the same tune

## Le gouzi-gouzi

On met la main droite en l'air
On met la main droite par terre
En l'air, par terre, bouge le derrière
On fait le gouzi-gouzi et on tourne en rond
Frappe les mains et crie youpi

**Refrain:**

Ohé le gouzi-gouzi !
Ohé le gouzi-gouzi !
Ohé le gouzi-gouzi !
Frappe les mains et crie youpi

On met la main gauche en l'air …
On met le pied droit en l'air …
On met le pied gauche en l'air …

Illustration © Anna Godwin / Beehive Illustration

- The children walk '*en farandole*', one behind the other, their hands (initially) on the shoulders of the person in front. The leader leads them around the room in a snake-like line, twisting in and out. The leader then shouts: *Le petit Limousin dit : main sur la tête !* The children then move their hands to the head of the person in front. So it continues with the leader's command changing at the end of each chorus to *sur l'épaule* (shoulder), *sur la hanche* (hip), *sur le genou* (knee) and *sur la cheville* (ankle).

## La danse du Limousin

Et nous allons danser
La danse du Limousin
Et nous allons danser
La danse du Limousin

**SCHOLASTIC**
www.scholastic.co.uk  Photocopiable

# Glossary

## Around the classroom

*ardoise* (f) . . . . . . . mini whiteboard
*bibliothèque* (f) . . . bookcase
*bic* (m) . . . . . . . . . . ballpoint pen
*cahier* (m) . . . . . . . exercise book
*calculette* (f) . . . . . calculator
*cartable* (m) . . . . . . school bag
*chaise* (f) . . . . . . . . chair
*ciseaux* (m pl) . . . . scissors
*crayon* (m) . . . . . . . pencil
*fenêtre* (f) . . . . . . . . window
*feutre* (m) . . . . . . . . felt pen/board pen
*gomme* (f) . . . . . . . rubber
*livre* (m) . . . . . . . . . book
*ordinateur* (m) . . . computer
*placard* (m) . . . . . . cupboard
*porte* (f) . . . . . . . . . door
*poubelle* (f) . . . . . . bin
*règle* (f) . . . . . . . . . ruler
*salle* (f) *de classe* . classroom
*table* (f) . . . . . . . . . table
*tableau* (m) *blanc* . whiteboard
*taille-crayon* (m) . pencil sharpener
*tapis* (m) . . . . . . . . carpet/mat
*trousse* (f) . . . . . . . pencil case

## Around the school

*dans notre école* . . in our school
*il y a* (un/une/des)
. . . . . . . . . . . . . . . there is/are (a/some)
*bibliothèque* (f) . . . library
*cantine* (f) . . . . . . dining room
*centre* (m) *de documentation et
information* (CDI) . library (usually with
computer facilities)
*couloir* (m) . . . . . . . corridor
*cour* (f) . . . . . . . . . playground
(*nouvel*) *élève* (m/f)
. . . . . . . . . . . . . . . (new) pupil
*gymnase* (m) . . . . gym
*instituteur* (m) . . male primary school
teacher
*institutrice* (f) . . . . female primary school
teacher
*réception* (f) . . . . . . reception
*salle* (f) *de classe* classroom
*salle* (f) *des profs* . staffroom
*terrain* (m) *de sport*
. . . . . . . . . . . . . . . sports field

## Classroom instructions and questions

*assieds-toi/asseyez-vous*
. . . . . . . . . . . . . . . sit down
*baisse* (z) *la main* lower your hand
*écoute* (z) *bien* . . . listen carefully
*fais/faites le geste* do the gesture
*ferme* (z) *la porte* . close the door
*lève/levez la main*
. . . . . . . . . . . . . . . raise your hand
*lève-toi/levez-vous*
. . . . . . . . . . . . . . . get up / stand up
*ouvre* (z) (*la fenêtre*)
. . . . . . . . . . . . . . . open (the window)

*regarde* (z)-*moi* . . look at me
*répète/répétez* . . . repeat
*tais-toi/taisez-vous*
. . . . . . . . . . . . . . . be quiet
*Un, deux, trois ... montrez-moi !*
. . . . . . . . . . . . . . . One, two, three...show
me!
*C'est juste ?* . . . . . . Is that right?
*Qu'est-ce que tu fais ?*
. . . . . . . . . . . . . . . What are you doing?
*Qu'est-ce que c'est ?*
. . . . . . . . . . . . . . . What is it?

## Clothes and school uniform

*chapeau* (m) . . . . . hat
*chaussettes* (f pl) socks
*chaussures* (f pl) . shoes
*collants* (m pl) . . . . tights
*gilet* (m) . . . . . . . . cardigan
*jupe* (f) . . . . . . . . . . skirt
*maillot* (m) *de bain*
. . . . . . . . . . . . . . . swimming costume
*pantalon* (m) . . . . . trousers
*polo* (m) . . . . . . . . . polo shirt
*sweat* (m) . . . . . . . sweatshirt
*uniforme* (m) *scolaire*
. . . . . . . . . . . . . . . school uniform
*Pour aller à l'école je mets ...*
. . . . . . . . . . . . . . . For school I put on/
I wear...
*Je n'ai pas d'uniforme*
. . . . . . . . . . . . . . . I don't have a uniform
*Je mets ce que je veux !*
. . . . . . . . . . . . . . . I wear what I like!

## Colours

*blanc* (he) . . . . . . . white
*bleu* (e) . . . . . . . . . blue
*brun* (e) . . . . . . . . . brown
*couleur* (f) . . . . . . . colour
*gris* (e) . . . . . . . . . grey
*jaune* . . . . . . . . . . . yellow
*marron* . . . . . . . . . . brown
*noir* (e) . . . . . . . . . black
*orange* . . . . . . . . . . orange
*rose* . . . . . . . . . . . . pink
*rouge* . . . . . . . . . . . red
*vert* (e) . . . . . . . . . green

## Common courtesies

*Bonjour* . . . . . . . . . Hello
*Bienvenue* . . . . . . . . Welcome
*Comment ça va ?* . How is it going/how
are you?
*A toute à l'heure* . . See you later
*Au revoir* . . . . . . . . Goodbye/see you
soon
*Bonne nuit !* . . . . . . Goodnight!
*S'il te plaît/s'il vous plaît*
. . . . . . . . . . . . . . . please

## Days of the week

*lundi* . . . . . . . . . . . Monday
*mardi* . . . . . . . . . . . Tuesday
*mercredi* . . . . . . . . Wednesday

*jeudi* . . . . . . . . . . . Thursday
*vendredi* . . . . . . . . Friday
*samedi* . . . . . . . . . . Saturday
*dimanche* . . . . . . . . Sunday

## Expressing facts and opinions

*J'aime* . . . . . . . . . . I like/love
*Je n'aime pas* . . . . I don't like
*Il/elle aime* . . . . . . . He/she likes
*Il/elle n'aime pas* . He /she doesn't like
*J'adore* . . . . . . . . . . I love
*Il/elle adore* . . . . . He/she loves
*Je déteste* . . . . . . . . I hate
*Il/elle déteste* . . . . He/she hates
*Je préfère* . . . . . . . . I prefer
*J'ai* . . . . . . . . . . . . . I have
*Voici ...* . . . . . . . . . Here is...
*C'est ...* . . . . . . . . . It's...
*Ce n'est pas ....* . . . It isn't...
*beau* (m) . . . . . . . . beautiful
*belle* (f) . . . . . . . . . beautiful
*difficile* . . . . . . . . . . difficult
*génial* (e) . . . . . . . . great
*grand* (e) . . . . . . . large
*intéressant* (e) . . . interesting
*laid* (e) . . . . . . . . . ugly
*moche* . . . . . . . . . . ugly/horrible
*petit* (e) . . . . . . . . . small
*super* . . . . . . . . . . . great
*avec* . . . . . . . . . . . . with
*donc* . . . . . . . . . . . . so
*et* . . . . . . . . . . . . . . and
*maintenant* . . . . . . now
*ou* . . . . . . . . . . . . . or
*parce que* . . . . . . . because
*pourquoi ?* . . . . . . . why?
*seulement* . . . . . . . only

## Ideal school

*cabane* (f) *dans les arbres*
. . . . . . . . . . . . . . . tree house
*fauteuil* (m) . . . . . . armchair
*fontaine* (f) *à chocolat*
. . . . . . . . . . . . . . . chocolate fountain
*piscine* (f) . . . . . . . swimming pool
*piste* (f) *de ski* . . . . ski slope
*skatepark* (m) . . . . skate park
*terrain* (m) *de golf* golf course
*toilettes* (f pl) *de luxe*
. . . . . . . . . . . . . . . luxury toilets
*trampoline* (m) . . . trampoline
*mon école idéale* . my ideal school

## Maths

*plus* . . . . . . . . . . . . plus
*moins* . . . . . . . . . . . minus
*fois/multiplié par* . times/multiplied by
*divisé par* . . . . . . . . divided by
*angle* (m) . . . . . . . . angle
*carré* (m) . . . . . . . . square
*cercle* (m) . . . . . . . circle
*côté* (m) . . . . . . . . . side
*forme* (f) . . . . . . . . shape
*hexagone* (m) . . . . hexagon

*rectangle* (m)..... rectangle
*triangle* (m) ...... triangle
*Je suis quelle forme ?*
................. What shape am I?
(*Deux plus trois*) *font* (*cinq*)
................. (Two plus three)
make (five)

## Months of the year

*janvier* .......... January
*février*........... February
*mars* ............. March
*avril*............. April
*mai* .............. May
*juin* ............. June
*juillet*........... July
*août*.............. August
*septembre*....... September
*octobre*.......... October
*novembre* ....... November
*décembre* ....... December

## Parts of the body

*bouche* (f) ....... mouth
*cheville* (f) ...... ankle
*derrière* (m) ..... bottom
*dos* (m) ......... back
*épaule* (f)....... shoulder
*genou* (m)....... knee
*hanche* (f) ...... hip
*main* (f) ........ hand
*nez* (m) ......... nose
*œil/yeux* (m (pl)) . eye (s)
*oreille* (f) ........ ear
*pied* (m)......... foot
*tête* (f) ......... head
*gauche* .......... left
*droite* .......... right

## Prepositions

*à côté de* ........ next to
*dans* ............ in
*derrière* ......... behind
*devant* .......... in front (of)
*sous* ............ under
*sur*.............. on

## School rules

*Il faut ...* ........ You/one must...
*être poli* ........ be polite
*lever la main* ..... raise your hand
*respecter les autres élèves*
................. respect other pupils
*Il ne faut pas ...* .. You/one mustn't...
*crier en classe*.... shout in class
*manger en classe* . eat in class
*On peut* ......... We/one can
*jouer au foot* ..... play football
*aller aux toilettes* . go to the toilet
*s'il est nécessaire*. if it's necessary
*Tu peux* (*lui*) *expliquer les règles ?*
................. Can you explain the
rules (to him/her)?

## School subjects

*anglais* (m)...... English
*dessin* (m) ...... art

*éducation* (f) *religieuse*
................. RE
*français* (m)..... French
*géographie* (f) .... geography
*histoire* (f)....... history
*informatique* (f)... ICT
*maths* (f pl)...... maths
*musique* (f)...... music
*sciences* (f pl) .... science
*sport* (m)........ PE
*Quelle est ta leçon/ta matière préférée ?*
................. What is your favourite
lesson/subject?

## Telling the time

*Quelle heure est-il ?*
................. What time is it?
*Il est* (*une*) *heure* . It's one o'clock
*Il est* (*trois heures*) *et demie*
................. It's half past (three)
*Il est* (*quatre*) *heures et quart*
................. It's quarter past (four)
*Il est* (*cinq*) *moins le quart*
................. It's quarter to (five)
*Il est* (*deux heures*) *dix*
................. It's ten past (two)
*Il est* (*deux heures*) *moins dix*
................. It's ten to (two)
*Vingt heures trente* 20.30
*midi* ............. midday
*minuit*........... midnight

## The school day

*après-midi* (m) ... afternoon
*déjeuner* (m) .... lunch
*devoirs* (m pl) .... homework
*emploi* (m) *du temps*
................. timetable
*matin* (m) ....... morning
*récré* (*ation*) (f)... break/playtime
*C'est quel cours ?* . Which lesson is it?
*C'est* (*les maths*).. It's (maths)
*L'anglais, c'est lundi matin*
................. English is on Monday
mornings

## Writing and spelling

*accent* (m) *aigu* .. acute accent
*accent* (m) *grave* . grave accent
*alphabet* (m)..... alphabet
*B majuscule* ...... upper case B
*b minuscule* ...... lower case b
*c cédille* (f) ..... c cedilla
*circonflexe* (m)... circumflex
*consonne* (f) ..... consonant
*graphisme* (m)... handwriting
*lettre* (f)......... letter
*mot* (m) ........ word
*voyelle* (f) ....... vowel
*Voici l'alphabet français*
................. That's the French
alphabet
*Epelez votre prénom /nom de famille*
................. Spell your first name/
family name

## Verbs

*aller*............. to go
*boire* ............ to drink
*cacher*.......... to hide
*calculer* ......... to calculate
(*dé*) *couper* ...... to cut (out)
*courir* ........... to run
*crier*............. to shout
*dessiner* ........ to draw
*écouter*.......... to listen to
*écrire* ........... to write
*être* ............. to be
*faire*............. to make/do
*frapper* ......... to clap
*jouer* ............ to play
*manger*.......... to eat
*nager*............ to swim
*parler* ........... to speak
*plier* ............ to fold
*porter* ........... to wear
*prendre*.......... to take
*respecter* ........ to respect
*toucher*.......... to touch
*tourner* .......... to turn
*voler* ............ to fly

## Vocabulary from games and songs

*champignon* (m).. mushroom
*chat* (m) ........ cat
*enfant* (f)........ child
*femme* (f) ....... woman/wife
*fermier* (m)...... farmer
*fromage* (m)..... cheese
*marron* (m)...... chestnut
*moulin* (m) ...... windmill
*noix* (f) .......... nut
*nounours* (m)..... teddy
*nourrice* (f)...... nursemaid
*oiseau* (m) ...... bird
*pantin* (m)....... puppet
*peluche* (f) ...... soft toy
*poisson* (m) ..... fish
*pomme* (f)....... apple
*pré* (m)........... meadow
*souris* (f) ........ mouse
*'Jacques a dit'* .... 'Simon says' (literally
'James said')
*Touchez la table* .. Touch the table
*Fermez les yeux* .. Close your eyes
*Ouvrez les yeux* ... Open your eyes
*Cache le lapin* .... Hide the rabbit
*Où est* (*-il*) *?* ..... Where is (he)?
*Où suis-je ?*...... Where am I?
*Montrez-moi !*..... Show me!
*en l'air* .......... in the air
*par terre*......... on the ground
*gouzi-gouzi*....... tickle, tickle /
hokey-cokey
*éliminé* .......... out (of the game)

**SCHOLASTIC**

# Also available in this series:

ISBN 978-1407-10203-0

ISBN 978-1407-10207-8

ISBN 978-1407-10208-5

ISBN 978-1407-10206-1

ISBN 978-1407-10205-4

ISBN 978-1407-10204-7

To find out more, call: 0845 603 9091
or visit our website www.scholastic.co.uk